RAVE REVIEWS JUST KEEP POURING IN!
EVERYBODY LOVES THIS BOOK!

MLM MAGIC

"MLM Magic — My favorite book on network marketing. It's easy to read and oh, so true!"

— *Ray Cassano*
Double Diamond Distributor, Cell Tech

"A sensational, easy-to-read and often humorous book about a very serious topic — MAKING MONEY! Venus Andrecht makes it clear to the reader what it takes to be successful in this wonderful business. Don't skip a page!"

— *Howard Meredith, Ph.D.*
Educator and MLM Entrepreneur

"Venus covers all the bases, shares the brass tacks, and gets to the nitty-gritty of multilevel marketing in a way that keeps you laughing all the way to the top. Her book has made a difference in my *life*, not just my business. I share *MLM Magic* with all my associates—upline, downline, and crossline—and highly recommend everything Venus writes."

—*Mary Saunders*
Gold Associate, Alliance USA

"Informative, straight talk on MLM, yet inspirational and fun to read. I really relate to this story."

— *Barbara Wyatt*
Wylink, Inc.

(continued on page 275)

MLM*
MAGIC

*MULTILEVEL MARKETING

HOW AN ORDINARY PERSON CAN BUILD AN
EXTRA-ORDINARY NETWORKING BUSINESS
FROM SCRATCH

Venus Andrecht

Editor – Summer Andrecht
Cover Design – Summer Andrecht

RANSOM HILL PRESS
P.O. Box 325
Ramona, CA 92065-0325
1-800-423-0620

619-789-0620
Out of U.S.

Margaret L. McWhorter
Ransom Hill Press
P.O. Box 325
Ramona CA 92065-0325
1-800-423-0620
619-789-0620 out of U.S.
619-789-1582 (fax)

Seventh Printing

Author – Venus Andrecht
Editor – Summer Andrecht
Cover Design – Summer Andrecht

ISBN: 0-941903-07-9
Library of Congress Catalog Card Number: 91-61552

DEDICATION

Dedicated to all of you who are ready and willing to do what it takes to change your position in life.

ACKNOWLEDGMENT

My thanks go to my company, my upline, my downline, and even my sidelines. Many thanks to all of you who have helped and inspired me as I rebuilt and changed my life through MLM.

My thanks extend even to the friends and family members who challenged, ridiculed or rebuffed me; it made my climbing muscles stronger.

And, of course, a big thank-you to my mother, Margaret McWhorter, who got up at 4:00 a.m. to put this book together, and my daughter, Summer Andrecht, who edited me (sometimes to the nerve) and designed the cover.

Love,

Venus

FOREWORD

When Venus Andrecht asked me to endorse her new book, I was thrilled! Venus is MLM's role model, mentor, teacher and special friend. Her book is an acknowledgment of her willingness to share and contribute back to people. I believe, as most networkers do, "Whatever you give out comes back." This book is an example of this principle.

Venus shares, discusses and strategizes with you, the reader, on how to be successful through developing an MLM business, as well as having you think about your lifestyle needs and sense of commitment. Her honesty is refreshing. Anyone who reads this book will alter their way of doing business. This book is a must if you want to gain and keep the competitive edge through MLM.

The future is now; career change is upon us and this book will provide you with the "magic" formula for your success!

Much Networking, Sharing and Prosperity,

Anne Boe

Anne Boe
Keynote, Motivational Speaker
Author of *Is Your Net-working?*

Contents

Boat • How Not to Approach Distributors • Don't Set People Up • Here Are a Few Things That Big MLM People Say Will Do You In When Approaching People • Those Other *Rotten* MLMs • Sincerity Wins • How to Set Appointments with Prospects • Selling Yourself • Following Up • How to Physically Sign Someone • Complications

Who to Choose • The Ideal Types of Distributors • Ideal Qualities in Prospective Distributors • Examples of Qualities That Succeed • Special Types AKA: Dysfunctionals • Revenge • Caution! • Gray-haired Marvels • Entrepreneurial Types • Learning to Discriminate • Be Selective • Sort People into Piles • Sometimes Discrimination is Not Easy • What About Those People You Already Have? • Who to Help, Who to Let Go • Blind Luck • Your Character • Hope Won't Do It • Seeing Through Your Preconceptions • Getting Over Negative Beliefs About Selling • Step Outside Your Circle • Selling is Sharing and Caring About the Other Person

Oh My Gosh! I Finally Signed Someone! Now What?! • MLM as an Art Form • Back to School • Depression • What to Do with New Distributors Immediately • Another Way to Say the Same Thing: Draw Up a Blueprint • What Happens When You Don't Train? • Miscellaneous Notes • There's a

Visualizing and Writing a Plan • Ideas to Build My
MLM Business This Year • What I Need to Earn
Monthly This Year, and Why • Ideas to Build My
MLM Business This Year • Your Physical & Mental
Health and Other People's Rules • Another Mind-
saving Device: Hired Help

PROLOGUE

IMPORTANT – WARNING

This is a totally honest, realistic look at how to build an MLM/networking business — from scratch. There's no powdered sugar in any chapter. There's no spun fluff, no get-rich-quick hyperbole or frenzied proselytizing. I'll never promise that after you join a company, all you'll have to do is invite your friends to lunch, sign them up, and then the lot of you will roll merrily to MLM meetings once a week, forever after — except when you're on your yacht in Tobago. I will, however, tell you what no one else tells you.

Too many people see MLM as the fast road to gold. Well it is the road to gold, but for most of us it's slow. It grows very slowly in the beginning (usually the first two to three years), and that's where the majority of people fail. They get frustrated, thinking, "Everyone else is doing so well so quickly. I must be a failure." Then they quit. Too often MLM companies, and the distributors within them, are guilty of "extension of reality." Perhaps Uncle Fud Riley makes a $2,000 bonus one month because he signed up all his dead relatives and bought 200 cases of product in their name. He's then written up in the company magazine as a success story, "Making $2,000 a month!" Then there's

Sally Firt, your sponsor, who declares earnestly and with a sweet face, eyes turned to Heaven, "This is so easy! All I do is talk to my friends on the phone and I earn $50,000 a month! You'll love this business!" She neglects to tell you that she's been involved with multilevel since she was six, and all the friends whom she calls and recruits have been working MLM with her since she was twelve. They're all trained and ready to hop like summer fleas into the latest viable MLM with Sally.

This book is written for you, the person who knows that MLM can be started with a minute amount of money, and has the potential for eventually rolling you in gold leaf. It is a business that has almost no risk — except your time and your sanity. This book is for you, a person who may have little or no training in MLM, but is willing to do what it takes to succeed.

I've written MLM Magic to help you stay sane and undaunted while you're in training, and to keep you calm as you sit through all the meetings where hype is blown around you like confetti. I want to help you stay in the game when everyone you know in the business is either telling you how rich they're getting and how easy it is, or how poor they're getting and how no one can make it. For you to persevere in multilevel/network marketing, you need to know honestly how bad it gets, how good it gets, and what it really takes to make it in MLM.

Let's start with how good it gets — what MLM can do for your life.

The Good Life

Several years into my present MLM, I've arranged life to my satisfaction. My favorite part is waking up about 7:00 a.m. If the sun is shining brazenly through my window, I get real excited. Either way, my old cat and I tumble down the stairs together. He eats breakfast while I uncover the birds and brew up tea. Then, we race upstairs again and both of us hop into the featherbed. Tomi purrs and talks while I sip tea, listen to classical music, and read something inspirational for my mental health. Sometimes I write. Sometimes I just drift and plan my future.

The second time I flounce out of bed, though, is when the work day starts. I go full thrust all day, doing whatever pleases me. I work, but I also make sure to go to fun places several times a week. Yesterday, my daughter, Summer, and I had a lobster lunch, then spent the afternoon in a funky furniture shop. Several days before, I spent two hours at a French Cafe, eating snails and buttered bread. In a few days, I'm going to my brother's restaurant where a radio show will host local celebrities: Molly Butterbreast who dresses like a chicken, and my mother, who reads palms and tea leaves.

A few weeks ago, I said to myself, "Hey, let's spend the afternoon with old folks." I went to a seminar on living trusts. This guaranteed that almost everyone was over seventy, and a lot were older. I just wanted to do something different — and it sure was.

There were about one hundred fifty old people in the room, all seriously figuring how to outwit the government. A lawyer fellow, about thirty, hopped about and explained very slowly and loudly that basically, they should, just sign their assets over to the young folks. One old man with a tag on his sweater marked "Roger" kept bellowing, "Hey! I can't hear you! Speak up!" He repeated his request every two minutes. Toward the middle of the class, a fellow about forty-five came in, half dragging his frazzel-headed old father. They inched their way along for about fifteen minutes, finally choose two chairs at the back and sat. The father immediately tipped out of his chair and rolled on the floor. I was horrified. The other old folks barely gave him a glance.

"Speak up, for God's sake!" Roger yelled. "There's so much racket back here I can't hear a damn thing!"

If you're still working nine to five, do you have the time and freedom to sample other slices of life? I think I've succeeded fabulously at learning to enjoy myself, and think it's great that we entrepreneurs have time to enjoy the odd parts of life. Of course, I can take vacations anytime I want — for whatever length of time I want. I have complete control over all of my time. I have the income now to be able to take my daughter with me on trips, so sometimes she and I will get a whim to visit Nebraska, or drive to New Mexico for a week, or fly to Vancouver, or to Montreal and the East Coast to watch the leaves turn color in the fall. These trips are also a business writeoff, because somewhere in my downline of distributors there is someone I can visit in any of these places. If, however, I don't have a distributor in a certain state or country that we're visiting, if I introduce someone to my company's products while I'm there, the trip can still be written off.

My Life Now

My life wasn't always like this. I'm a single mother who, before MLM, had lived in genteel poverty. What a change MLM has made for me. My first year in MLM brought me approximately $150,000, and I didn't understand half of what I was doing. That same year, I went from a rental condominium to my own beach house, bought two new cars for cash, and among other things, I bought a pile of undented cooking pots and matching silverware. I was also awarded a $24,000 bonus and trip to Hawaii for being the second fastest growing MLM group in my company (the top winner consisted of a corporation of eight people). I also made a batch of solid friends and earned respect and confidence in myself, and the knowledge that my life could, indeed, improve.

All this happened because I was desperate, and because I believed in the company and its products. It happened because I took a chance, ignored all the obstacles, and persevered. I worked out of my kitchen the entire time (and still do), generally in my jeans and bare feet.

That first year, I made no cold calls, didn't advertise, and made at the most only two formal, sit-down presentations. There wasn't much I did the right way, because I didn't know what right was. I'd been fortunate enough to have had some schooling in network marketing five years before, but was unfortunate enough not to have made any money, and had retained only a few contacts. What I did learn and retain was the knowledge that you have to work at MLM. When everyone in my new MLM was boasting about how well they were doing, how much money they had rolled up in their pants, how many people they'd signed, and how *easy* it was, I didn't believe a darn word of it. I knew what I'd have to do and laid out my plan, which is presented throughout this book.

Who I Am

Four years into my present MLM, I find myself lounging on my balcony, surrounded by boxes of pansies, ranunculus, and daisies. I've just watered them, so as I sit here on my outdoor carpeting, my rear is wet. But, what do I care? I'm glad and grateful to have the time and money to watch my eucalyptus tree shaking its fingers in the sky, while singing its rustle-leaf tune. I'm so happy. Maybe I was always happy and never noticed it because I was so busy trying to corner the next few dollars.

I no longer care about the next few dollars. I don't need to care. After about one and a half years in my business (and for many people that's two to three years) I began to realize that I couldn't stop the money if I tried. It would be pointless to tell you what I make a month now, not only because it's so outrageous, but because it keeps going up every month. Let's just say it's in the high five figures.

You're going to read about all the hard times I had getting here. You need to know about them, but I no longer care! Purely on the material end, I now own two houses, an acre of land, two cars, health and accident insurance, investments, a retirement fund, and have money in the bank. For the first time ever, I'm able to replace the bath towels from my first marriage, have a nice tea set, more than one vase, pants that fit, and frankly, any damn thing that catches my attention. What a novelty!

However, the most important thing that MLM has given me is freedom. If I want to sit for days and think about the error of my ways, or the salvation of my soul, I do it. If I want to recline in my organic garden from sunrise to sunset, I have no guilt while sitting. Every morning I wake up and thank God and the universe because, first, I don't *have* to get up, and second, I don't have to merge on those freeways! My day isn't planned and apportioned out; I can do anything I want with the next twenty-four hours. Nobody tells me what I should do or how soon I should do it. Sometimes people solemnly tell me, "Money doesn't bring happiness." Just as solemnly I say, "It sure has for me." It's given me my life. Before, I was living to survive. Now, I'm living to enjoy. Before multilevel, I was trapped in a box.

Now those walls have collapsed and I have time. Money buys time. Time to notice and enjoy the seasons, time for me to talk to Summer, to surprise her with gifts, and take her places. There's time now to sit with my animal friends, and time to paint, to write, and to cultivate and enjoy friendships. MLM brings friendships because it's packed with people. I just pick and choose.

I've also traveled more in the last four years than I've ever traveled in my life. Multilevel companies practically beg people to earn the exotic trips they dangle under your nose, so, what can I do? I win them.

My life now is a matter of choosing. The choice is, "Now that I have plenty of money, am well traveled, have lots of friends, and have my freedom, what do *I* want to do with the rest of my life?" If that's a question you'd like to eventually ask yourself, read on, and learn how I made the leap for freedom into a new way of living.

INTRODUCTION

Life Before MLM:
What It's Like Living in Genteel Poverty

It was a hot, dusty day. My mother and I were bouncing around town together, just gadding about. Mom was driving down Main Street, while I hung my head out the car window, looking for air. Suddenly, I heard an inner voice. It said, "Go see Diane." What the heck?! I pulled my head back in the window.

"Mother," I said, "let's go see Diane." Mom looked startled, but agreed. I felt startled myself. I hadn't seen Diane, an old friend of mine, since I'd left Ramona two years before. I hadn't even thought of her. I'd been too busy, living "down the hill" by the ocean, trying to make a living for my daughter and myself.

Five years earlier, my life, never dull to begin with, had taken some interesting and unsettling turns. I'd gotten a divorce and lost so much that I had to return to my hometown to live. My daughter, Summer, and I had settled into a tiny house on my parents' ranch while I adjusted and recuperated. A year later, driven by financial need and hoping for excitement, we'd headed into the "Big City" to build a new and, hopefully, better life. My second marriage and divorce had, finally, peeled off much of my naiveté and most of my hard-earned financial assets. I'd always owned my own house, but was now reduced to renting. My car was a sweet Datsun 280ZX, but it was also ten years old. I hadn't bought new clothes for a long time, and we ate the cheapest foods available. Luxuries of any type were never a consideration. Luxuries included health, life and renter's insurance, movies, books, and meals out. Money was so difficult for Summer and me that my tax-preparer refused to charge me. We existed below poverty level, for reasons only other single mothers in America can fully understand. I wasn't lazy; I'd had my own successful business before the divorce. However, my ex-husband now owned it, along with an injunction saying I couldn't recreate the business nor do similar work for a number of years. (He was afraid of the competition.) I could have gone back to teaching, but the pay and conditions were abysmal.

My close friend at the time, a nice steady fellow named Buck, kept insisting that I get a "real job." A "real job" to him meant nine to five, five days a week, with a steady (but minimal!) paycheck. Buck became like hot water dripping on a largely unresponsive stone, "Get a 'real job.' Get a 'real job.' Get a 'real job.' " He harassed me so much that when he decided I should become a school bus driver, I actually fell in with the plan. It wasn't until I was filling out the forms that I came to my senses. Believe me, my inborn talent was not directing me to be a school bus driver! The kids wouldn't have wanted me, either. It was at this desperate point that the words, "Go see Diane" dropped into my perspiring head.

On the way to Diane's, Mother and I discussed her. Diane was the tired grandmother who had grandchildren to raise, a goat dairy to take care of, and an herb business to manage.

"That poor girl," Mother said, "she needs a rest. She's so exhausted that when I go there for herbs, she can't even get out of her chair. When I tell her what I want she waves limply toward the shelves and says, 'They're over there.' She's just got too much to do."

Fate Takes a Hand

What a surprise we were in for. No limpid lady came to greet us at the door, but a vibrant new woman, looking ten years younger and jumping around like a teenager.

"Diane! What in the world have you done?" we asked.

That's all it took to pop her lips loose. My friend immediately and eagerly, not to mention enthusiastically, began to sell me on her new product and multilevel marketing business.

Then Diane's husband, Al, came dancing into the room — another transformation. He was so sold on this product that he was giving up his secure job with the fire department to help Diane with her new business. Now here were the two of them, rattling on about this new product...*ho hum.*

I was amazed by their transformation, but still had no interest in yet another multilevel marketing plan. Actually, I had less than no interest. I'd been in a multilevel five years before. In fact, the multilevel was the very business I'd lost to my ex-husband. It was a good MLM, but a hard one. In that particular networking business it had been darn difficult to make any decent money. Once out from under the burden, I'd determined to stay away from multilevels forever.

But now, as I sat in Diane's house, an absurd thing happened. I began to feel an Invisible Hand on my right side, on the small of my back, pushing me toward Diane. (At this point, you may be exclaiming, "Oh, oh, I knew it, Marge! Venus is a weirdo! I knew it the minute I saw her name! I'm not reading this book!" Well, just keep in mind that this nut, a few years later, makes a generous five-figure income *per month* because of that Hand on her back.) I was puzzled, of course, by the feeling. It was distracting. Diane was hopping and jumping about, flashing her teeth and extolling the virtues of her newfound product. This wasn't like Diane. Diane was a laid back chair-sitter. Mother knew this about her and watched with fascination, while I, attempting indifference, kept twisting in half circles looking for the person behind me!

Now, here was Al, a quiet type, I'd thought. He, too, leapt into the MLM dance, grinning and flailing his arms in the air, chanting out the virtues of their incredible new business.

"Well," my mother ventured when there was a pause in the stream of hallelujahs, "I've *never* seen you two act like this. If you think it's that good, I might as well try your product. Give me a bottle."

My mouth dropped open. My mother?...being taken in by a scam? Impossible! I was even more surprised when I heard the words that rolled out of my own mouth. "I'll take a bottle, too."

I didn't want a bottle! Why did I say such a thing? I sank back into the chair as Diane prepared to release us from our money. As I watched, peeved and perplexed, an odd thought came into my head, *"She's going to make money off us."*

"Wait!" I heard myself shout. "I'll sign up!" Mother looked at me as though my brain had fractured. Perhaps it had. All I knew was that if I signed up, we could get the product cheaper. Of course I never intended to buy it again. Nor would I ever, *ever* sell it or make a business of it. But for some unknown ridiculous reason, I wanted to spend more money signing up than I would have if I'd just bought the darn bottle. All eyes were on me. The Hand pushed me forward. I signed the forms, paid my money, and looked Diane and Al straight in the eye. "And...don't think," I said, "don't you think even for a minute that I'm going to do this business!"

Then, my mother, the Invisible Hand, and I flounced out.

I Did It — So Can You

Several years later, in spite of my former reluctance, my entire life has radically changed. I have become a wealthy woman through multilevel. The story that follows is how I did it...and how you can, too.

MLM, or Multilevel Marketing, AKA: Network Marketing

What It is, Who It's for, and Why

I never wanted to join a multilevel. A lot of people feel that way and I think it's because we don't know any better. We have a leering, sneering attitude toward multilevel marketing that has been fostered by some pretty rotten MLM companies. Then, of course, there's the obnoxious distributors we've run into. One guy laughingly told me this story: "Whenever I want the jacuzzi all to myself in my apartment complex, I just run into the crowded spa room, hop in the water, grin, stick out my hand and shout, 'Hi! I'm Greg! I'm your local _____ representative, and I want to tell you about our latest, greatest product!'" He says the folks fling themselves out of the water like fruit flies and take off.

So why would you want to become an MLMer? Lots of reasons. To own your own life, for one. Consider this: At age sixty-five, only 5% of us can retire without Social Security. And those of us on Social Security average about

$775 per month. What kind of life is that? That's what you get after forty years of working for someone else. That's if you don't get fired before that, of course. Wouldn't you like to have more control over your own life? There's a way to do that, and it's called multilevel.

Did you know that many millionaires created over the last ten years came from multilevels? How would you like to be one, and why not?

More and more products and services are being sold thru multilevel. People like to bypass the middle person to buy quality products, at a better price, from friends who stand ready to guarantee and service what they sell.

With MLM (like me), you can be your own CEO! I sit in my kitchen office and feel just like Lee Iacocca.

Plan it right and you can quit the rat race and join the human race, which I think was just made for sitting outside all day in a field of flowers, drinking tea with friends.

And tax writeoffs! I went to a tax seminar a while back. The speaker was an ex-IRS agent, and he absolutely waxed lyrical about having an MLM business. He shouted that people are fools —*fools* to work "real jobs." With our kind of work, every trip is a tax writeoff! Would you like to visit Hawaii? Or even Alabama? Just have distributors there, or go and find some and write the trip off. Any place you love to vacation can be business. And, closer to home, let's say you still have that "real job." You have to drive back and forth to work every day, and there's no writeoff there. But, get a post-office box along the way, for your MLM of course, and because you pick up the mail on your way, the drive is...deductible! Remember though, tax laws change. Stay informed.

What Is MLM, or Multilevel Marketing, AKA: Network Marketing?

Over the years, MLM has gained a rancid reputation. Disreputable companies and people have prostituted the concept to the point where people are afraid of it. When MLM is mentioned, many people think, "Oh yikes! Pyramid! Ripoff! Scam! Run fast!"

Because of this, MLM has a lingering aroma quite repugnant to people who don't know the true nature of this creature. Realizing this, enterprising MLMers have adopted a new word for MLM; they call it *Network Marketing*. They explain that the reason for the new name, is because the concept is a combination of both multilevel marketing and direct selling. To me, it looks the same as it's always been. But, what the heck, by any name it's an incredible deal.

MLM, or, Network Marketing, has been around for quite awhile. Amway and Shaklee are some of the old-timers. Many other major corporations, including telephone companies, are now joining the ranks. Why? Because this form of moving products works — in a big way. A *very* big way!

Look what happened to me, a single lady working mainly out of her home, in jeans and bare feet, who is making more than most executives and doctors. How can this happen? MLM makes it easy for you to have a business of your own, starting with little money and little risk. First, choose your product and company carefully. Then, build a network of distributors who distribute your company's product. Profits come from direct sales and money (or royalties) earned on sales made by your network of downline distributors.

This is vastly different from traditional marketing of

products. When you buy radishes from the grocery, for example, those radishes have been handled by a lot of different people. Beginning with the farmers who raise the product, the radishes then get passed to the wholesalers (the jobbers) and distributors. The wholesalers and distributors then pass them to the retail people, and the retail people rent the space from the building owners to get the radishes to you. Meanwhile, advertisers are hired to create hoopla which supports sales of the product — which supports all those people it has taken to get the product to you. Often, the inherent integrity of the product is lost in the shuffle, and you, the consumer, must rely on word of mouth anyway to determine which is the best product to buy. You usually end up taking a friend's opinion over a television commercial! (These commercials, if you haven't noticed, often hire people who look like your friends, your children, your parents, and your doctor — all giving you free advice about the worthiness of the product!)

In MLM, the company creates the product. They rely on you to get it directly to the consumer (your friend, your neighbor, your children, etc.). And soon, instead of the profit being split between all the people conventional marketing requires, it now goes directly to you and your distributors (again, your friends, your neighbors your church, your children, etc.). This method often keeps the product less expensive and of higher quality. (After all, no one would tell their friends to see a bad movie or buy a bad product.)

How to Recognize a Good MLM Company

The following important points are taken from an article by Jeffrey A. Babener, an attorney in Oregon, who specializes in multilevel marketing. It appeared in the September 1990 issue of *Money Maker's Monthly*, a newspaper for MLM people. Because of the potential for abuse, multilevel has become a tightly regulated business. Here are some points to consider when selecting an MLM company to join.

Consult Your MLM Lawyer

Network Marketing Vs. Pyramid Schemes

© September, 1990 by Jeffrey A. Babener. All Rights Reserved

1. The Product or Service. The company should offer a high quality product or service in which consumer satisfaction is guaranteed. It must have a "real" demand in the marketplace. If the product is consumed by the distributors themselves, it must be one that distributors would want to buy on its own merits, irrespective of participation in the marketing plan.

2. Price. The price of the product, or service, must be fair and competitive, be reasonable, and competitive with other similar products in the marketplace. Distributors should be able to purchase the company product at wholesale or at substantial discounts from prices found in retail stores.

3. Investment Requirements. There should be no investment requirement except a sales kit or demonstration material sold at the company's cost.

4. Purchase and Inventory Requirements. A legitimate marketing plan should have no minimum purchase requirement, nor any inventory requirement, for one to become a distributor or sales representative. Once in the business, however, ongoing activity or qualification requirements are typical of leading network marketing companies.

5. Use of Product. Products should be used by consumers and not end up in the garage or basement.

6. Sales Commissions. Sales commissions should not be paid for the mere act of sponsoring other distributors.

7. Buy-back Policy. A legitimate multilevel marketing company will agree for some reasonable period of time to buy back inventory and sales kit materials in re-salable condition from distributors who cancel participation in the program.

8. Retail Sales. The focus of the marketing program should be to promote retail sales to non-participants. Many states and programs recognize that purchases for personal or family use in reasonable amounts by distributors are also retail sales.

9. Distributor Activity. Many of the new statutes regarding multi-level Distribution companies require that distributors provide a bona fide, supervisory distributive selling or soliciting function in moving the product to the consumer, i.e., that they have meaningful contact and communication with their downline sales organization.

10. Earnings Representations. The basic rule is that a legitimate marketing program should not make any earnings representations unless those representations are based on a track record. Testimonials by individuals of their own experiences are not uncommon.

11. Training. A good network marketing program should offer solid training in sales and recruitment to its distributors.

The future of the network marketing industry will require cooperation by companies, distributors and those governmental agencies charged with regulating the industry to assure that legitimate practices prevail and pyramiding schemes are stamped out. Every network marketer should apply the above principles in evaluating a new program or working within their existing programs.

Biographical Information: Jeffrey A. Babener is a partner in the law firm of Babener & Orcutt, One Main Place, Suite 600, 101 S.W. Main, Portland, Oregon, 97204, (503) 226-6600. Mr. Babener is a graduate of the University of Southern California Law School and a member of the editorial board of the University of Southern Law Review and has served on various state and American Bar Association committees, including the chairmanship of the Oregon State Bar Committee on Judicial Administration. His legal practice includes representation of many of the major companies in the direct selling industry. Sales by companies he represents exceed $2 billion involving over one million distributors. His law firm represents companies headquartered throughout the United States and abroad. He represents many members of the Washington D.C. based Direct Selling Association where he serves on the Lawyer's Council and Government Regulations Committee and he is corporate counsel for the industry's other trade association, the Multi-Level Marketing International Association of Irvine, California. Mr. Babener has lectured and published extensively on multilevel marketing law. He has been interviewed on the industry in such publications as **Money, Inc.** and **Atlantic Monthly.** He is editor of the monthly industry publication, <u>Direct Sales Legaline.</u> Mr. Babener is also the author of the books, <u>Tax Guide for MLM/Direct Selling, Distributors, The Network Marketer's Guide to Success</u> and <u>The MLM Corporate Handbook.</u> He is chairman of the MLM Entrepreneur Conference Series, a nationwide series of conferences on trends in the MLM industry.

To Choose or Not to Choose

Since you're reading this book, you may already have chosen an MLM company. At this point, you may be uncomfortable about your choice, or perhaps you soon will be.

MLM Checklist

Go over this checklist before you invest in any MLM company:

MLM Checklist

☐ Do you use the product?
☐ Do you like it?
☐ Is the price reasonable?
☐ Would you buy it even if you weren't selling it?
☐ Is the original investment low?
☐ Is the product one that will sell?
☐ Will there be repeat business?
☐ Does the company have a buy-back policy with no minimum purchase required?
☐ Does the company have a good training program?
☐ Will you get adequate help from your upline?
☐ Is there good earning potential?
☐ Are earnings based on product sold and not on number of distributors recruited?

This checklist will give you an idea of how good your company is.

When I joined my first, and later my second, MLM company, I never thought once about the above mentioned rules for choosing a good company. I never even knew about them. Boy, was I lucky! Since then, I've been told horrendous tales about many other multilevels. Maybe you've heard about the companies that suddenly go under — leaving their distributors with garages full of product. Or, bang!, a company's monthly paychecks start bouncing. And we've all read about the companies that are closed down by the FDA or Attorney General. Then there are always the companies that have such a darn difficult marketing plan that only a few people make any decent checks. And what if the products a company sells are one-time items geared only for white women over forty with size five feet? What if the company president runs off to Tijuana with all the money?

It's no wonder regular people snarl, hunch their shoulders, and trot off when you mention multilevel. We have a bad reputation, but, wonderful companies do exist. Make sure you join one of those. It will save you much grief and work for naught.

"So," you may be thinking, "what's available out there? Where are all these wonderful companies for me to choose from?"

The best way for you to start your search would be to stand on a busy street corner wearing a sign that says, "Help! I want to join a great MLM company."

Passing drivers will throw themselves out of their cars and slap onto you like biting flies. Most nine-to-fivers have some little scheme they're working on to get them out of their miserable jobs, and if they don't, their cousin, wife husband, or mother-in-law does.

More realistically, just pass the word around that you're looking for a great MLM. Every night of the week MLM is operating in some home or hotel room. You'll never have enough time to hit them all. In fact, if people let you down by loving their nine-to-five jobs and don't know MLM from cat litter, then check the ads in the newspaper. Look under Sales or Business Opportunities. Call the numbers and plan to have every day and every evening booked. In fact, you might strangle and drown in the rhetoric spewed out by your city's vast horde of MLMers. It will be a unique experience.

Take a look at the different MLM companies and choose a few to look into which have products that you could be enthused about. For example:

1. Is plastic kitchenware your thing? How about cosmetics or midnight lingerie parties? What about water-tight faucets, or oil which lasts the life of your car? Are you into health products? What about brooms, pans, new diets or water? Somewhere out there, you'll find almost everything represented by an enterprising MLM company or two.

2. Ask yourself: "Are the products in my field of experience or knowledge? Does it matter to me if they aren't?" I have always been interested in health and helping others to live better, healthier lives. Because of this, I feel an urge to get my company's health products out to people, and that has made it easier for me to stay excited about my work.

3. Will you be representing something you believe in? Do the products or services work? Do they compare well with what is already available in the common market, or are they in a class all their own? You may want to take into consideration also that some companies are more charitable than others. Some have concerns about the environment, and

their products reflect that concern. The company I'm involved with has a foundation set up for children in need. It makes me feel good to know that I'm contributing to this cause as well as my own.

4. Demand to know what the company's objectives are. Are they a fly-by-night, get-rich-quick scam? Putting your faith in a company is a lot like buying stock in one. You'll want to know where the profits you earn for a company (similar to the investment you'd make in one if you were buying stock) are going. Is it into charities? Into expansion? Into debt? Into the hands of a small group at the top? Large companies as well as small ones offer unlimited possibilities for return from your investment, so long as they are sound. Just like buying stock, it's the growth and integrity of the company, as well as the resistance of the products to market fluctuations, which will bring in the returns.

5. Once you have applied the above points and limited your possible choice to a few companies, ask to see their marketing plans. If the companies are otherwise acceptable, the generosity of their marketing plan could be a deciding factor.

To further clarify what you are getting into, let's again look at other methods of marketing:

MLM versus Other Types of Marketing

1. Conventional Marketing: The use of national advertising campaigns is the generally accepted way large companies market their products. The individual retailers also advertise the product, hoping to lure people into their stores to buy the nationally advertised brands. If you are the retailer, you're dependent on employees and responsible for all the taxes that go with having employees. If you are the employee, you're dependent on a salary and can only make as much as your employer is willing to pay you.

2. Mail-order Marketing: We're all familiar with Sears and Montgomery Ward catalogs. There are other smaller companies that mail catalogs and/or flyers as their form of advertising. As in direct marketing and MLM, people with smaller companies often use their homes as bases of operation. Unless the company is very small, it will also have employees to be responsible for.

3. Direct Marketing: Direct Marketing is closer to MLM than any of the above types. Originally, most direct marketing companies sold door-to-door. Remember the Fuller Brush Man? Direct Marketing methods now have become more subtle. They may still go door-to-door, but are more likely to use the "party" method of selling — for example: Tupperware, Avon, and Mary Kay. They use distributors but usually do not concentrate on building a downline of distributors. This distinguishes them from multilevel marketing. Several of these companies are considering going multilevel, if they haven't already.

4. MLM/Network Marketing: The MLM company uses its money to motivate its distributors, *not* the national public, by:

- Improving the product.
- Adding new product.
- Supplying sales tools.
- Giving educational classes.
- Offering generous bonuses, royalties, trips, cars, and other incentives.

Most of the advertising in MLM is left up to the individual distributor. The distributor provides the retail outlet, usually his or her home. Finding and educating the customer is the responsibility of the distributor. With the help of the sponsor (the person who signs you into the company) the distributor (you) finds friends, relatives, and neighbors (known in MLM as downline) to share this new product and new business opportunity with. Your downline is composed of all the people with whom you have shared the product and who have signed into the company (becoming a distributor, like you) and all the people that these people have shared the product with and signed into the company and so on right on down the line. One leg of your downline is one of your distributors and the downline of this distributor. (See diagram on the following page.) Remember, the distributor is an Independent Contractor and responsible for his own taxes.

If all the details I'm tossing at you are confusing, ignore them. Personally, I didn't understand numbers, or legs, uplines, downlines, or even the marketing plan when I began my business. I just went out and sold the product, and sold the people, on the opportunity.

The Marketing Plan Diagram

This diagram should help explain the basic structure of network marketing. It helps to think of multilevel as family, with each generation helping and leaning on the other.

Think of multilevel as a family. Each generation helping and leaning on the other

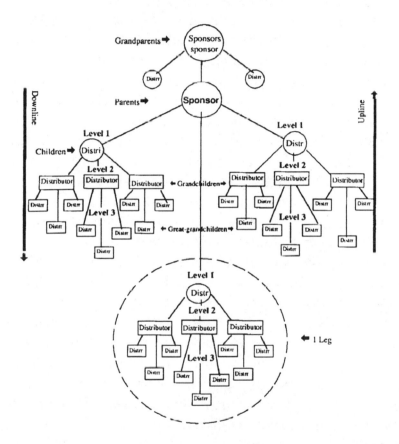

Every marketing plan will be different, so we're just generalizing here. Also, the titles: *Sponsors, Distributors, Managers, Supervisors,* may all be different.

As you can see, Sponsors are Distributors who have signed other Distributors below or under them. Distributor and Sponsor are almost synonymous, because a Distributor becomes a Sponsor every time he/she sponsors someone into signing into the company. Sponsors are considered as being at the top of their *downline* (a parent to some, a grandparent to others, a great-grandparent to still others, etc.), and their responsibility is to all those under them. Similarly, the Sponsor was sponsored by someone also, and so forth, on up the line. These people are called your *upline*. Again, everyone who either you or your distributors have signed are called your *downline*. All these names may be different in your particular MLM.

By meeting certain qualifications within your company, you will become a Manager, Supervisor, or whatever your company calls the advanced folks. It is generally at this level that you will begin earning royalties (a percentage of every bottle, case, box, or whatever, that is purchased from the mother company) from all the product that your downline moves. This is where the big money is. Getting to this level is relatively easy in most companies, and your sponsor should eagerly be giving you all the details.

Most MLM companies will show you various ways of earning income by moving their products. Know the difference between a *Retail Customer* and a *Distributor*. Retail customers will buy the products from you, month after month, until they either move out of town or find a better product. You'll make a little profit off each bottle, box, or wingnut you sell them.

Distributors are people you have signed into the business under you (exactly the same way you were signed up) who either know they'll be purchasing the product for a long time and want to get it at a discount, and/or are serious about building a business. If you want to make it BIG in MLM, you will concentrate on finding business-building people like yourself who want to earn their freedom by becoming a Distributor like you.

Your initial goal should be to become a Manager, or Supervisor, or whatever your company calls you when you reach the level where you begin earning royalties from the sales of the Distributors underneath you. Your plan also includes having as many Managers or Supervisors as possible, because their increased income also increases your royalty income, while relieving you of the work.

Although my diagram shows downline for only three levels (beginning with the Sponsor), the actual marketing plan can go from three to five levels deep, or more, depending on the company. At three levels, you receive royalties from the sales of your downline to the third level (great-grandchildren) where your royalties stop. At five levels, royalties are paid on the sales of your downline five levels deep, and so on. Some companies have a roll-up effect, where unproductive Distributors or Managers are skipped in each leg and you are paid as far down in a leg as it takes to find your three or five levels worth of productive Managers. By simple mathematics (say, you sign up five people who all become Managers, and each of those five sign up five people who all become Managers, who each sign up five others, and so on...), you could easily have over 3000 people in your downline at the fifth level.

Of course, it rarely works this easily. Some people sign up to buy product for themselves and their families. Some buy for themselves and to sell to a few friends. Some move, drop out, or die. However, just a few people under you who work hard can earn you a lot of royalties. In fact, many MLM magnates earn 95% of their wealth from as few as four active legs.

To recap, in MLM you earn money in at least two ways. First, from the product you sell (retail sales). Second, on the product sold by the people under you (in the form of royalties). You are not rewarded for the number of Distributors you sign up, only for the income they generate.

Is MLM for You?

Now that you know something about MLM, you need to ask yourself, "Is it for me?" Entrepreneurship requires certain qualities. It's possible to acquire them if you are properly motivated. For example, desperation is a prime motivator that will speed you along while you're learning. It certainly did in my case.

You need to note what you have going for you, and what you will need to work on.

A Touch of Genius Is in Order

Every one of us has at least a little bit of genius stuck in our noggins. In order to find it, start by identifying your natural abilities. These are the qualities that come easily to you. To do this, you may have to think way back to when you were three or four years old.

Consider some famous dancers, musicians and artists. They were talented to begin with, but then kept using their talent, growing and expanding, until they became the best in the world in their field. The same thing is true of fine architects, outstanding teachers, or big business tycoons.

As children, the architects may have liked to build sand castles and slap boards together. As they grew older, they just kept doing it. The terrific teachers probably always taught their dolls, their parents, and other kids. Business tycoons most likely started selling lemonade, candy bars, pencils, and raffle tickets before they even had teeth to brush.

The main key to success here is that these people, consciously or unconsciously, identified their natural abilities and used them constantly until they became superior in some way.

What comes easily to *you?* Can you use these qualities in MLM to your advantage and eventual success?

Your Natural Abilities

When you were a kid, what did you like to do? What came naturally? Once you remember these personal quirks, all you have to do is use them or do them...over and over, until you're so adept in those areas that you're judged a genius.

Take a sheet of paper and list the things you've enjoyed doing and have done well over your lifetime. It's fun to do this. To give you some ideas, I'll use myself as an example.

As a kid, I came in with the following: I liked to draw. It came easily to me, and I drew all the time. I was also introspective, thoughtful, and responsible. I liked to dig swimming pools. My folks just let me dig until the holes got too big, and then they'd use them for trash and garbage dumps. This offended me, but I kept digging. Revenge came, however, when my father swam in one of the muddy water-filled holes one hot summer day. That bit of pleasure brought him a big boil up his nose and another on his rear. And me? I got one on my knee, but kept right on digging.

Creativity

As a child, you probably had a wild imagination. It's time to go back and revive it. Here's what I came up with:

I had a talent for devising contraptions. I'd run thick ropes through pails, big wash buckets, metal pipes, chairs and anything else of interest. Then I'd wind them into the large tolerant elm tree in our side yard, generally with some kind of pulley. Next, these devices had to be tested, preferably with a human being in the bucket. My youngest sister still carries a scar straight down the center of her chest from one of my experiments. That particular ride flipped her upside-down, nose first into the ground. She quit riding, but I kept building and testing.

Entrepreneurship

Surely you had a lemonade stand. Almost every kid has had one, or they at least sold Girl Scout cookies. Maybe you did something more interesting. Here are some more ideas from my background:

Since we were a family of eight, and there wasn't much money, it was imperative that I earn my own. By the first grade I was drawing and selling paper dolls to my classmates for ice-cream money. Of course, there was the Cheery Cards episode (this follows later), just one among many. I was born enterprising, and, because of necessity, kept it up.

Persistence

Stick-to-it-ivness is another desirable attribute in multilevel. Your folks probably called it stubbornness. Whatever it's called, it gets results.

To me, a multilevel business is just another kind of pool or spinning wash tub that I'm putting together, that will work one way or another. I keep taking the business apart, then fitting it together, trying different things until I find the pieces that work. And, I don't give up. If I'd given up when I was a child, there wouldn't have been anything to do! We lived in the country, so I became naturally good at keeping myself amused, and that's what I do today. Building a business keeps me entertained.

Resourcefulness

Resourcefulness is another important quality. This is something you may not realize you have until you need to use it. As you will see shortly, my resourcefulness was tried to the utmost when I went to Singapore to expand my business.

Add It All Up

How does all of this fit into my MLM success? From earliest childhood I had to think and be creative in order to amuse myself and have a few pennies in my handkerchief. I found it easy to spend time thinking about what I wanted and how I'd get it. A natural inclination was used repeatedly until I got darn good at it. I also seemed to have a sense about how to plan things, and then execute them. This, of course, was an ability that I repeated over and over with new types and kinds of swimming pools and hanging tree devices.

The Singapore Experience

I'm including this story as an example. Of what? Resourcefulness, persistence, creativity, entrepreneurship — all of these qualities were brought into play during my attempt to sign up Singapore. Hopefully, you can think of some experiences of your own which will help you to see these qualities in yourself, because MLM requires them.

It was my inborn enterprising self that went to Singapore three days after I decided I should be there. My current MLM was opening in that country. After several months of thinking that that was the last place I'd ever want to go, I just got up and went.

Summer, 18 years old, came with me, not by choice, but

out of duty. "I can't let you go by yourself, Mom!" she said. "You'd be all alone there, a single woman in a place that doesn't seem to respect women in business, and thinks that a woman isn't a woman without a husband!"

What? No Husband?

So there we were, not one, but two business women without husbands, traveling alone in a third world country. I was told that if I was bold enough to go, I should take a man with me and let him do all the talking and the doing while I hung back and played secretary. I had been strongly advised that I'd get nowhere in a man's world if I faced the Singapore people as a successful woman.

I was darn nervous and shy about my lack of prudence, but as soon as Summer and I got over the culture shock and jet lag, we had to face a few facts. It did seem to be a world of men. On the whole, their business tactics and ethics were quite different from ours. So different, in fact, that I spent one entire afternoon in the hotel bathroom crying and almost accepting the fact that I would go home a failure. Almost, I say, because that's when my natural enterprising center asserted itself. We'd wasted a week feeling trounced and overwhelmed by polite, loving, warm-hearted men whose business practices had peeled our skin right to the bone.

Where's Your Husband?

"Where's your husband?" was the first question every man asked me.

"I don't have one," I'd say. Eyebrows would lift.

"Where's your father?" they would ask Summer.

"He's in the U.S." she would blithely answer.

"You're here...alone?" they'd gasp.

By that time we were wondering about that folly ourselves! But, to heck with being an inferior woman who should have stayed at home steaming rice while praying for a husband. And to heck with that single status. I advertised our MLM in the local paper and interviewed in our hotel room!

The steady stream of men hiking up to our suite must have been the hotel scandal — two single women far from home, entertaining strange men in their bedroom. I didn't care. We had work to do.

For the week previous, I had presented the business as I always did in America, "This is the product, this is the opportunity, are you interested in being involved?" Most Singaporeans loved networking and wanted to do the business, and after I'd spent the afternoon convincing them of that fact, they happily signed up...with their friend, cousin, sister, auntie, or man in the hotel kitchen! Why should they sign with me, a woman and a foreigner who would soon leave them to their own devices?

Resourcefulness Pays Off

I thought about it. Belatedly, I realized that *I* was the answer — the *reason* for them to sign with me. In the States I was quite modest. Here, I needed to be extraordinary. So, I was. I trotted out all my credentials and flung them on the table. Fortunately, I'd brought a copy each of my first two books. Hauled out, they were casually, but effectively received.

Next, I laid out a copy of my company's magazine, the one with me on the cover, of course. I briefly told my story: "In my first ten months, I made $100,000 working out of my kitchen office. At the end of my first year in the business, I purchased my own home. I also paid cash for two brand new cars, paid off a piece of land, bought bookcases, a toaster, a picnic basket, and a college education for my daughter. A year before, we had been living in genteel poverty."

During this self-presentation I strove to look exceedingly bright, business-like, and sure of myself, while remaining warm and casual.

Sometimes You Have to Blow Your Own Big Bugle

"And," I finished up, "the product and company are quite new in this country. Anyone you might sign up with won't know much. I know a lot. I've been in the business three years and know all the right people. I know how to run an international business." Then the capper. "I have books, flyers and other training materials that aren't available in your country. I'll get them to you when you sign with me. Plus, I travel quite a bit, and will be back to see you. So..." I'd say as I pulled out the distributor application, and handed them a pen, "what do you want to do?"

One evening, I'd worked for an hour on one man. He just couldn't decide if he wanted to sign up with me or not. He'd swing one direction, and then another. I extolled my personal virtues until I was bored with myself, but he still couldn't decide. Finally, in exasperation, I said, "Nic, just sign the darn thing!" I wrapped his hand around the pen and pushed the paper up against his stomach. "I have to be at a meeting and can't wait any longer." He looked at me and signed.

"Come on," I said, "come with me to the meeting. We'll start right now getting you trained. Pick up that kit for me. Thanks. And please get that pile of stuff over there."

I trotted toward the door. "Boy, I'm thirsty!" Reaching into the hotel's refrigerator, I pulled out two bottled waters.

"Want one?" I asked. He did. I handed one to him and proceeded to try to open mine. I realized we needed a bottle opener, and didn't have one. I thought a moment, then smacked my bottle against the wall, knocking the cap off. Nic still struggled with his. I watched his feeble attempts for a few moments, lost patience, snatched his bottle, and in one rolling sweep whacked it against the door jam. The lid popped off and flew across the room.

"O.K.," I said, "let's get a move on." Nic looked at me with reverence.

"You are the most enterprising woman I've ever met!" he breathed. My inborn abilities, used constantly, had paid off once again.

Now It's Your Turn

Take a blank piece of paper, sit in a quiet place, and ask yourself, "What comes easily to me?" Then, ask your mother, "Mom, what was I like when I was little? Tell me the kind of person I was and what I liked to do. What was I good at?" You may have to suffer through a pile of baby books, clay hand prints, pewter baby shoes, and maudlin sentiment, but it should be worth it. It could make you a million dollars...or more.

Also, think of experiences you've had which have tested the abilities that I listed earlier.

Turn the page and fill out the form. Find a quiet spot and be honest with yourself as you rate your abilities and assess your qualities.

Then go over your list. Can you work for yourself? Are you willing to push yourself to the utmost to build yourself a future?

Rate Your Abilities

1. Natural Abilities:

2. Creativity:

3. Entrepreneurship:

4. Persistence:

5. Resourcefulness:

Commitment and Company Loyalty

I Know What I Can Do — Now What Do I Want This MLM to Do for Me?

Now you are aware of the components of a fair multilevel networking business. You can see the potential in yourself to be successful in one. Now you will need to ask yourself, "What do I want this MLM to do for me?" It's important that you take a piece of paper and write out what you're working for. Are you building this business so you can pay for your father's spare set of false teeth? Or to get out of debt? Or to be wealthy enough to be thought eccentric instead of crazy? You need to remember these things when you want to quit the business. When what you're working for is taped to your refrigerator, your bathroom mirror, and your dinner plate, it will be easy to remember that yes, you absolutely need money to afford these things, and that MLM is the only realistic way to get them. Here's the list I wrote when I was first building my business. I asked myself, "What do I want this business to do for me?"

My Wish List

1. I want MLM to give me my personal and financial freedom. That is the most important thing in the world to me. I never want a nine-to-five job again.

2. I want to live my own life. I want to get up every morning and think, "Wow. What do I want to do today?"

3. I want money so I can come and go as I please. I want the mobility that money brings. No more scrimping and saving. No more having to be places I don't want to be, doing things I don't want to do.

4. I want to be able to sit outside all day and every day if I wish. No more teaching school in cold prisons without windows. No more being constantly on call for real estate clients. No more tearing here and there, ruining my health for other people.

5. No more relying on other people for my life and livelihood.

6. I want to be free to be the person I really am and to do the things that make me happy. That means I can:
   - Write more books...without feeling I can't afford the time.
   - Counsel people...without worrying about making a living.

- Have a peaceful, happy life, with time for friends and family.
- Notice and enjoy the seasons and spend time with nature.
- Make $2,000 to $3,000 a month, so I can easily pay all my bills. (Of course, that modest wish expanded way beyond my dreams...but I was open!)
- Own a house of my own.
- Send Summer to college.
- Buy a new car.

Think about this list. What do you need and want in life? Is there any other way for you to get these things? Do you know of any other way in which you can consistently double your monthly or yearly income? Realistically, will you win the lotto or will your rich Aunt Jane die soon and leave you her heirloom china that will sell for $125,000 a plate?

Will that handsome rich man really ride into your life and gift you with his personal fortune? Or, will he make you sign a prenuptial agreement? Do you have another means for obtaining money besides working for it through MLM? Or do you just need enough money so that you can do what you've always wanted to do? Things like painting, becoming a world-class jet-skier, or riding bare bottomed on a burro through South America writing travel columns?

Turn the page now and make *your* wish list.

Your Wish List

1. Personal:

2. Family:

3. Financial:

4. Social:

5. Intellectual:

6. Spiritual:

7. Just plain fun:

Take your list now and tape it to something you see every day.

Making Your Commitment

After you've carefully chosen your company and made the list of what you're working for, the next important step is to make a commitment to yourself. Once I realized what I'd fallen into with my MLM, I got serious.

"For one solid year," I told myself, "I will work this business night and day. I'll start working it at 7:00 a.m.— I'll work it around my real job and I'll work it until ten or eleven at night. Whatever it takes, I'll do it. No matter how discouraged I get, no matter what's not happening, no matter how many times I make mistakes, I'm not quitting. In one year, I'll reevaluate. At that time, I'll decide if I should continue."

Once I made myself that vow, I couldn't break it. If I had, I would have lost respect for myself. Thank goodness I made that commitment. If I hadn't, I would have quit twenty times — minimum.

How will you know that you're firmly committed? If you're thinking about your new business night and day, there's a strong possibility that you're committed. If you're making lists, setting goals, and following through, that's another good sign. It's especially promising when you don't let discouragements and depressions flip you end over end.

I knew I was committed when I found I was dreaming about my company and products every night. It got so intense for a while that one night I was stunned when I had a dream inside a dream. There I was, pushing cases of product through another totally unrelated dream! That's the kind of commitment I mean when I say: *"Make a Commitment."*

Put the Rest of Your Life on Hold

This may sound excessive, but it worked for me. Timing is everything. No matter which MLM you choose, and no matter how you look at it, if you start now, you'll be farther along than you would be later. If it's a solid company, it's going to last and will still be there when you're ready for it. But it may also be in every state, and many of your contacts will already be involved. Putting off committing simply wastes time. You will lose time waiting for your kids to start school. Waiting for your girlfriend to decide you're the man for her. Waiting for your husband to give you permission, waiting for the money from Uncle Willy to come through so you can start the business — there are always valid reasons why the timing isn't right. You could wait your whole life.

When I started this business, I put many things aside. I write books, and had two in the works, but I shoved them under the bed. "Soon," I said, "I'll have so much money, I'll be able to write those books in all my free time."

My special friend, Buck, resented this business. When he was around he tried to forbid me to answer the phone. He called my week-ends his and planned trips to get me out of town. He let me know he thought I was foolish to think I could make more than a little money off MLM. I, rather quickly and maybe callously, tossed Buck aside.

I didn't consider anyone a friend who would try to stop me from reaching my goals, or who wouldn't take me seriously and support me in my efforts. Children, of course, can't and shouldn't be put aside, but Summer was in step with and supported me. She knew she would benefit, too, and so she didn't begrudge me the hours I worked. I gave up free time, the time I'd formerly used to read books and go out to lunch. Anything else that was distracting or not in line with my goals I modified or put away for a while. And it really was only for a while. In two to five years, you too can haul out the things that are still salvageable and roll in them if you want to. You'll have the time and money to do it.

Don't Expect It to Be Easy

People look at me now and say, "Gee, it was so easy for you." No, it wasn't easy! You should see my appointment book for the first year. I was revved up and ready to go. My motors were racing and smoke was blowing out my nose. But...?

My Tattletale Appointment Book

1988

Jan. 2: I have written: *"Tried to call the company to order product. Nobody answers!"* Of course not, I realize now it was a holiday!

Jan. 3: I've penned in *"See Henry for lunch. Sign him up!"* (Henry had signed me into my former MLM, and I knew he'd sign with me now. He had a huge downline and would be my ticket to freedom.) At the lunch, Henry made it clear he didn't have a dangle's worth of interest in my new program. He told me he'd agreed to lunch only to get me back in his!

Jan. 4th: This day was blank. I think I was recovering from my naiveté.

Jan. 5th: *"Go to a company meeting. Write down gas mileage."* (I knew that someday I'd need those writeoffs.)

Jan. 6th: *"Ditto."*

Jan. 7th: *"Ditto."*

Jan. 8th: *"Ditto."* I'd drive anywhere, talk to anyone, observe anyone's meetings to learn about the business. (Nobody was going with me, either. I didn't have anyone to take!)

By **Jan. 9th** I was penciling in, *"Give Product and Business* Meetings." You've got to remember that I didn't have one distributor and I didn't know much, but I figured I knew more than some. What better way to train myself than to just hop in and help give meetings for other people's groups?

Next in my book, you'd notice many blank pages. I was talking to people, making phone calls and writing letters, but getting no response. I was getting discouraged. But I'd made myself a promise, remember? I couldn't break it. I referred to my list of what I wanted MLM to do for me. I knew that without my MLM I had no future. My life would remain the same. The bills would get paid, but there would be no money for extras. How would I send Summer to college? What if I got sick? How would I ever retire?

The thought of getting married for security, and relying on a man's goodwill scared the pa-diddle out of me. Having no money meant never being able to live my life the way I wanted to.

I Stick to My Commitment...

...against great odds, with no money or business success — yet.

My friend Buck, who was still with me at that point, continued to natter me, instructing me to get a "real job."

MLM didn't sit well with him. Looking him smack in the eye I'd say, "I know I'm going to make it. I'm going to do really well in this business. I'm crazy about the company and the product, and I'm going all the way." Sensible Buck would breathe heavily, roll his eyes, and go out and pound nails in his fence.

January rolled on. By February, Buck was gone, but I was still hard at work. Rolling rocks up MLM hills. Looking at my appointment book I notice that toward the end of the month, I'd started writing in the names, addresses, and phone numbers of the people I'd approached. Looking at them now, I remember the grief that went with each one.

One couple was in my previous multilevel. I knew how difficult it was to make money with that company. I thought my friends would be delighted to hear from me since I'd found something that helped people and tied right in with what they did. I knew that they'd be delighted—especially since this company was much easier and vastly more lucrative than their current one.

After I breathlessly explained the program to them, they told me where to hop off. People don't like to feel they've wasted their lives with the wrong company, can you imagine? Many of the names on those pages responded the way I had, at first — with vast, bottomless indifference.

One lady even snapped at me, to my continuing bewilderment, "Does your ex-husband know what you're up to!?" When I admitted that he didn't she snorted, "Well! Then I certainly wouldn't be interested!"

February slid into March. I was selling some product. Actually, quite a bit of product. Probably, the harassment these people were getting from me was doing the trick. "For God's sake Martha. Buy a damn bottle so she'll let you off the phone!"

Success at Last...Sort Of

I think it was somewhere in March that I got my first distributor. I shook with excitement as she signed up, and bought a *case* of product! Penny and I were both elated. She was going to build a business and finally make her husband proud and respectful of her. I was going to get my business off the ground. After a morning's worth of training and hallelujahs, she trundled to her car, a child slung under one arm, another kid trailing behind, and the product in the stroller. The next day she was back, teary eyed and red-faced with the case in her arms. Her husband wouldn't let her do the business.

I remembered my commitment. "No matter how discouraged I get, no matter how bad it looks, I'm sticking with it and working relentlessly for one year."

The months that followed were pretty much the same. What was working for me were the sheer numbers of people and a *can't quit* attitude. Gradually, I retailed more and more product, and from that culled a few distributors

Maybe I should mention the quality of distributors. Most were flighty. Some never did a thing, just disappeared in the breeze that blew up overnight. Others snailed along for a while, then dropped out. Some bought lots of product, made a great deal of noise, popped a big flare, and then extinguished themselves. Others bought a bit of product, signed up a few people, and just kept a hand in.

I made quite a bit of retail and wholesale money. Not much came in from managers in the form of royalties. Most of my income came from bonuses my company gave for volume purchased by my fledgling group and me. The first time I got one of those bonus checks ($2,300), I had to call my upline to see why. I still hadn't mastered the marketing plan. All those little circles hanging off of sticks on the chalkboard still confused me.

In my sixth month, a lady whom I'd pursued since day one finally got fed up with my nagging and joined me. She was solid in the business. For the first time, I felt as if I might really get somewhere. I'd found an ace.

Success at Last...for Sure

Ten months into the business, I'd earned a lot of money. How did I do it with such a rocky start? I sold a lot of retail and earned some royalties. I also earned some very generous bonuses, including one for $24,000 (even though I still didn't quite understand how I got those bonuses, because I still didn't entirely understand the marketing plan)! This just shows you that the attributes you need in the real business world don't necessarily mean much in multilevel. Being confused hasn't held *me* back. If you're waiting until you understand all the intricacies to make your commitment or get started, don't wait! You might miss your $100,000.

Company Loyalty
AKA: a Man, His Wife, and His Girlfriend

Now that you've committed to your company, be a faithful spouse. Infidelity brings pain and divorce. With divorce you lose many assets and, worst of all, you have to start all over.

Every time I sign up a new distributor, I advise them to stick with us and no one else, and I tell them why. If they follow another siren's song, they generally learn, as Jake and Vicky do in the following tale, that the siren tends to lead them over a cliff and into the sea.

Jake and Vicky

There was a terrible flap in my MLM today. The word

was passing around that a manager couple in my downline had joined another MLM company.

This is no ordinary couple. They blew into the business with a background of wealth and big business. Charming, convincing, beautiful people, they rallied a great group of distributors around them.

In a short time, they had garnered some of the top company prizes. They had dazzled quite a few people in the company—including some of the company's big stars who had been involved in various MLMs for twenty years or more. This couple could do things that normal people couldn't. They were able to talk to strangers on the street and sign them up cold. They generated an internal excitement in their group and were expanding so fast that the rest of us marveled. Then, the ridiculous happened. They joined a second MLM company and began stuffing their people into it.

Now, according to them, they had two sure-fire MLM companies. They thought this because they were still babies in MLM. They had come from another world, the world of big business. They had succeeded wildly out there. They were only doing what they knew how to do, that is, to hook two good things together and make a ton of money. But MLM doesn't work the same way that the rest of the business world works. MLM is different. Jake and Vicky thought they could run two MLMs in a spectacular way. Maybe they could, but their people couldn't. Their distributors became confused and began dribbling their efforts in two directions. Where once there had been a mighty river heading toward one point, there were now two smaller rivers going in opposite directions. When I discovered Jake and Vicky's defection, I spoke with them candidly, saying, "You're destroying your group. You're like a man with a wife and a girlfriend. At first it's heady and delightful. Then the wife finds out and hell hits the walls. You can't keep both and you may lose both."

Jake and Vicky disagreed. They explained that they'd had problems in our MLM. Because of this, that, and another thing, and because their group needed ready money (which the new MLM could supposedly provide), they'd signed on. "There's always bumps in the road with a new business," I cautioned. "I had plenty of my own, and still do. Work them out. Don't quit or look for an easier way just because you have difficulties building your business."

Jake and Vicky chose not to listen to me. They felt they knew how to be successful.

They didn't know, however, that MLM has the largest grapevine growing on earth. A week later everyone knew that the fabulous couple, their MLM idols, had been unfaithful. I immediately called Jake and Vicky and laid it out.

"You will be ostracized. No one will want your people around them or their group. They'll be afraid that their distributors will be infected by your distributors who are in the other MLM and will leave to join the other MLM." I explained to Jake and Vicky that they would have to choose one company over the other. I told them I wanted them with me, but if their heart was with the other MLM, to go to it, I understood. This devastated Jake and Vicky.

"We love all the people in this company," they said. "We've let down everyone who looked up to us. We thought we knew what we were doing."

"Look," I said. "You're not ruined. You're very human. You made a mistake because you didn't know any better. You're brand new at this. I bet everyone has tried running two MLMs at once. I have. I almost lost my group over it."

"Sit down and decide which MLM you want to be in. If

it's ours, let it be known to key people that you screwed up and that you have learned a big lesson. People will understand. They're human, too. They will respect you for owning up to your faults. I'll be with you all the way. I will help you however you wish."

"But," Jake moaned, "we've lost our group, Venus. Our distributors are confused, and some are still joining more multilevels — thanks to what we taught them. We've lost our status with everyone. We'll have to start over."

So Start Over

"So? Start over," I said, "I've had to do that, as have many other people. But remember, when things get rough, as they generally do, most people quit. Are you going to quit? Or are you one of those who runs through all odds and makes it to the top?"

"But, Venus," Jake said, "we hardly have anyone left who isn't confused or frustrated because of us. Everyone has dropped out."

"You should see my records from when I started this business," I said, "I can show them to you! Tons and tons of people who promised they'd make me rich — gone! Scores of people who swore undying allegiance to our products and company — gone! And quite a few people that I made mistakes with — gone. But in their place are others...people who stick. Which kind of person are you, Jake?"

It's Important to Keep in Touch

Here is another example. I was chatting one day with another distributor of mine, Della. We talked about Jim and Carole, the wonderful couple she'd signed under her. They'd been in our business for about six months and were doing extremely well. This was phenomenal because Della had never been in MLM before, and neither had Jim nor Carole. During the conversation, Della laid a lit stick of dynamite on me. Casually, she said, "Next weekend Jim and Carole are having a guy speak to their group about another multilevel."

"What?!" I yelled. "They're what?"

"Yeah, they've got a man in their downline who's involved with another company. One of these diet cookies. He's going to talk to their group about it. Want to come?"

"Why?" I blurted out. "Why in the world are they doing that? What's wrong with them?"

"Well, well, what do you mean?" Della squeaked, honestly perplexed.

"Are you are crazy? Have you split your marbles?" I snapped. "Why would you all even consider such a thing?" I already knew the answer. The three of them were so inexperienced they didn't know any better. Among other things, they didn't know about company loyalty being a major component of solid business building.

"Well," Della said, "we thought it'd be good to learn about other multilevels, and he's a nice guy. Maybe we could help him out?"

"Listen Della," I said, "you'll help him out all right. Your wonderful downline that you've worked so hard to build will sign and scatter. You'll shred them to bits. You'll lose your business. If people want to do cookies, that's fine, but for God's sake, don't point their nose at it and *force* them to leave you."

I went on like this for about twenty minutes, giving Della a crash course in multilevel. Finally, I decided I'd beat the juice out of it and let a shaken Della go. She was shaken all right. She said she'd call her downline immediately and educate them. Whew! It's important to stay in touch with your people. You never know what they're up to.

Jake, Vicky, and Della were all disloyal to their company out of ignorance. Jake and Vicky were never able to repair the damage, while Della lassoed her horses just in time. Be smart. Don't even get close to that position. If you begin to realize that you're in the wrong MLM, sit down and think it through. If you decide to leave — leave (but don't keep your left leg in your former MLM while you drag your people's right legs into the new company). If you are a distributor in several MLM companies because you buy the product for your own personal use and want to get it at a discount, that's one thing, but if you are considering building a business and selling the product to other people, choose only one.

Remember, if you split your energies, you split your power. You're like the mighty river heading toward the ocean that suddenly drains off into several or more creeks. You're still all heading toward the ocean, but much more slowly. How are you going to both go to and give more meetings? It's often difficult to get your downline to go to even one meeting every week. Why will they suddenly be willing to go to your "Bitsy Baby Booties" sales trainings every Saturday and your "Super Fly Trap" meetings on Sundays? You're doubling your work as well as theirs and they'll probably notice! It's easy enough to get discouraged when results are slow in coming...won't all of you find it doubly hard to stay motivated in two or more companies? How will you keep all the marketing plans straight? And how will you keep each company's flyers, tapes, T-shirts, videos, baseball caps, and products separate? My gosh, where are you going to put all the various inventories and how are you going to pay for it? Surely, you know that to reach your goals you have to stay focused on them. How will you do that with several different companies? Don't let greed run off with you and dance you down the double, triple, or quadruple MLM path.

You may have convinced yourself that eventually one of these businesses will take off and, then, that will be the one you'll work seriously with. But will your people decide that with you? By then, they'll be so confused and unfocused that you'll never be able to recapture and train them. What you'll have is a downline that believes they should constantly be looking for and joining other MLMs.

Think twice about being disloyal to your Chosen One. Infidelity in your personal *and* professional life brings pain beyond the pleasure.

Getting Started

Your MLM Work Journal

Have you ever kept a journal or a diary? Sporadically through the years, I've written in a few. They were full of my yo-yo-ing emotions, personal tragedies, and dysfunctional love life. Sappy books. They embarrassed me, so I tossed them in favor of starting what I call a work journal.

Through the years, I've often snatched up loose pieces of paper and written out my bills, how much money I need to make, creative ways of making this money, and so on. Then I promptly lose them. Years later I'll come across these scratchings. They're so intriguing. They have no dates, no outcome, nothing beyond the pictures of my mental workings of the moment. Awhile back, I found a yellowed page stuck in a book. I can only guess that it must have come from the years when I was married to Summer's dad, about twenty-four years ago:

Gas and electric – $3.00 a month
Food – $15.00 a month
Rent – $75.00 a month
Phone – $5.00 a month
Gas – $4.00 a month
Must cut back! Must make more Money!
What a laugh I had over that one!

Oddly enough, all these years later, I'm still making these lists, trying to cut back and make more money. But now I have a work journal. It's a regular hard-cover book with blank pages. The one I'm keeping at the moment is bright red (so I can't lose it) with flowers on the cover. I keep it close to me.

Whenever I have a thought about how to make this business grow, I write it down. The book is also a part of my morning ritual. It's close at hand when I wake up. Often, as classical music plays, I have an inspiring book in one hand and my journal in the other. The book I'm reading often sparks off creative ideas for my business — ideas that I immediately write down.

The journal contains anything remotely connected to my work life: bills, itemized lists of other people's checks (so I can keep a pulse on the beat of the business), items for future newsletters, thoughts about the company and its products, people I've suddenly remembered from twenty years ago that I should call, notes from business seminars, tax information, New Year's resolutions, etc.

I carry the book with me to meetings and training seminars in case I hear something that I want to remember. This book is a wonderful compilation of all the important undated loose notes I used to make and quickly lost. You might consider a work journal, too.

Appointment Book

For your day to day plans, you need to buy a big doctor's appointment book. Then, use it. Plan each day. What hours are for business? Mark them in. Who will you have lunch and coffee with? Who do you need to write or call? When are your days off? Keep your mind in that book. If your book is blank, then your MLM checks are probably nonexistent, too. However, if you're faithfully filling in that book and following through, those checks will come. Just remember; later on you'll get paid for all the work your appointment book is recording now.

You'll be surprised at what your *hourly wage* will turn out to be. Mine is now approximately $250 an hour for a thirty hour work week. And going up.

Getting Started

Now that you have your two workbooks and are ready to lurch ahead, let me give you a bit of direction.

Building an MLM business requires that you must *first train yourself.* Hopefully, your sponsor or someone in your upline is willing to share what they know with you and help you.

The key idea here is to realize that building your business and training yourself involves finding others (distributors) and training them to copy your actions. This means that your distributors are now scouting for people and training these people to copy them, etc., on down the line. If you help your distributor to sign a prospect into the business under them, you are helping yourself as well. Whatever income either of them generates will be reflected in your monthly check from the company.

To find people to train, the people who will *be* your business, you must create a prospect list.

The Prospect List

After I made the commitment to my company, I had to get down to work. Action had to be put behind the dreams.

I began my business the day I took out a legal-size note pad and began writing down the names of everyone I knew — all the way back to conception. Then I looked at them and thought, "Oh my gosh. Now I've got to call or write them." Looking over the list, I put checks by those who definitely needed a good opportunity in their lives. Next, I starred those who needed my products. If I had put a star and check by their name, I contacted them first. If I was using the phone, I just talked to them, like a regular person.

"I have to share something with you that's changed my life." I invited them to a get-together at my place, to lunch, or to come with me to a company meeting.

With those to whom I sent notes or letters I was just as informal. I wrote to them as one would a friend, enclosing a *small* amount of product or company information and promising to call them in a few days.

What happened next? Many people said, "No." Big fat "No's" that hurt my feelings. Others made excuses. Still others never returned my calls once they got the drift. Many humored me. Some had an interest. A few joined me in the business. Most didn't stick. However, it was a start. I knew that if my deck of cards had played out differently, I might have found an ace or two in that list of acquaintances.

Here's What You're Looking For

To start, you're looking to find three to five strong frontline people, although you'll want more later. These are people you will sign directly under you. Next, you will teach them to each find three to five good people to put directly under them. Then, you'll have them teach those people to do the same, etc., all the way to infinity.

I made a *long* prospect list. Following is that list, in abbreviated form, for the sake of space. (If you're new at this; you may have to contact and sign a large number of people to find your solid three to five. When you have more MLM experience, you'll find it easier to locate and choose the *right* people.)

My Prospect List

Family:
1. Mother — She may not go for it, but she'll be your ally.
2. Dad — You could run into a conflict here.
3. Sister Polly — On second thought, relatives may be a testing ground.

Best Friend:
4. Susan — She'll follow me wherever I go.

Acquaintances:
5. People from church.
6. My daughter's friend's parents.
7. Everyone on my Christmas card list.

Strangers:
8. The druggist.
9. The lady at the dry cleaner's.
10. Someone at the supermarket.
11. Someone I met pumping gas.
12. Etc.

Begin with the people you know best:

Your Prospect List

Family: 1.
2.
3.

Best Friend: 4.

Acquaintances: 5.
6.
7.

Strangers: 8.
9.
10.
11.
12.

A good sponsor, or let's say a sponsor who knows what he or she's doing, will help you with this list. (And remember, now that you're learning how, you will be expected to be a good sponsor, too. To be a good sponsor, and for your own benefit, you will help each of your new downline with their prospect list!)

Not only your sponsor, but the rest of your upline should be available to help you choose the best people on your list to contact first. You want to cut down on the number of those discouraging "No's" that people tend to give you at first. If from experience your sponsor can suggest those prospects potentially most receptive to your products and/

or business, you'll hear more of, "Yes, I'm interested."

Remind your upline that a distributor isn't properly sponsored until they have at least two to three good people who are signed under them. A distributor won't quit the business and leave if they have something to lose.

We'll go into detail in the next chapter on how to train and be trained, but right now your main objective is writing your prospect list. Without this list, there's no one to talk to about your exceptional business. No one to sign up, and no one to train. Put this fascinating book down, right now, and write *your* list.

Ideas for Finding Distributors

Tea, Talk and Tip Time

Yesterday, I had one of my little tea parties. Sometimes I'll invite the people in my group who need a bit of help to gather in my living room, drink tea out of flowered cups, and talk. The topic yesterday was "How to Find Potential Distributors." That afternoon, my brother Jim dropped by and was drawn into the discussion. Jim is an incredible salesman. He can talk to anyone. He has friends in all strata of society. Everyone loves him.

"Jim," I said, "share your secret. How is it that you're so popular?" He thought a minute before saying, "I'm interested in people. I never think about selling when I meet them. I get to know them first. We feel comfortable together. Then, if it strikes me that I have something they need, I tell them about it."

My forte, like Jim's, is that I feel friendly very quickly toward people. I can feel I'm friends with a person within just a few seconds or so, and introduce my business into the conversation without strain. As a rule, however, try to meet several times before you broach the MLM subject. Although often, as I was telling my tea friends, your connection to another person lasts only a few minutes. So I asked them to consider this instead: What harm is there in making the most of those few minutes if that's all you'll ever have?

Continuing on, I told them to become a joiner of just about anything, or become a civic leader, or just someone who helps mold the community in some way.

Paul (Yes, I invite men to my educational little parties!) told us that recently he had joined a local service club, looking for new blood. He's enthusiastic about his results. "Venus," he said, "you wouldn't believe it. I have eight legs now, and five of them came from that club. Three of those legs are exceptionally strong." (In case you forgot, a *leg* is one of your distributors and all of their downline.)

Find the movers and shakers in life and get to know them. These are the people who head the bowling leagues, run the PTA's, and organize the Scouts, Brownies, Bluebirds, and softball teams. They're the schoolteachers and people who are tired of working in real estate.

Spend time with the sociable people; they're the ones with many friends and interests. As you build a relationship with these people, it's easy to casually mention your line of work, and feel your way from there.

Other Ways to Find People

I've seen MLMers who tie their product around their neck and let it dangle! (I've never seen anyone with a water purifying unit around their neck, but I'd like to.) Some people wear a company button. I know *you* don't want to. I know that you'll feel like a fool, and maybe because of it you'll have to talk to someone. One day, Maggie, one of my downline managers, and I decided to meet for lunch. We just wanted to relax and have a jolly time. As we swept into the restaurant, the woman in the booth next to us gasped to Maggie, "Oh! I love your pin! What does it mean?"

That was the end of our quiet lunch. Finally, Maggie had to trip out to her car to get product and brochures. An hour later the woman left. Maggie snatched her button off and we ate in peace.

People are always asking me, "Where can I find serious distributors for my product? Everyone already takes it, uses it, sells it, or doesn't want it. It's too late for me."

Out trots the old story that you may know by heart, about Jesus Christ, the most famous MLMer. Two thousand years ago, He signed up twelve distributors. Christianity has been perking along ever since. They're still signing up new people, even though most folks have heard about Christianity (or Buddhism, Atheism, etc.), just as they may have heard about your product. However, these belief systems are still getting converts. These converts may even have tried the religion (or your product) before, but they didn't listen then, or care, or understand, or weren't ready. The point is: *Now* they are.

Churches, Schools, Charities

Speaking of religion, have you thought of signing up churches? They always need new roofs or more food for the poor, and bake sales don't bring in that much money. MLM can become a reliable money source, if all the parishioners use and enjoy the product(s). Begin by talking to the minister. Once he's signed up, become involved, and set up an account for the church, the parishioners will have faith and will sign under the minister.

Ralph, a fellow with a real estate background, called a few months ago, quite excited. "I contacted and signed the minister of an Hispanic church, Venus. He had me climb up on the podium and give a lecture about my products and company to the whole congregation. I was nervous, naturally, being *up there* behind the pulpit in the presence of God and all the brethren, but more than that, nobody spoke English! Some lady had to translate for me after every two sentences. I tell you, I got so befuddled I couldn't remember what I'd said before and what came after!"

Ralph told me he'd gotten to know some of the church workers. We're always looking for the workers in any group! They were impressed by how much money his MLM could make for the church, and a few of them signed up and bought an amazing amount of product!

Don't limit yourself to churches. Schools, charities, and organizations of all kinds need fund raisers. Your MLM will certainly make them more than a fudge sale would.

Retail Shops

Half or more of the retail businesses in the U.S. are struggling to survive. They pay thousands of dollars to work seven days a week and struggle. You've probably noticed that they're always going out of business. Big signs in their windows proclaim *Moving!* or *Remodeling!* or, just plain honest, *Quitting!* Some simply and quietly fade away.

Bob, a man in my company says, "Find the management person in a shopping center and take that person to lunch. Say, 'Let me know when people are going out of business.'" When he finds a failing retailer, he pulls on his dress pants and bounces into the store, clipboard in hand. He's a good-looking guy with an apricot tan. He flashes a smile and says, "Are you relocating? Expanding?" He is a friend to them and asks more questions like: "What do you like about this business?" He never, but never, hits them up about his wonderful, impossibly promising multilevel. He may, however, waggle his clipboard around and mention, "My partner and I are expanding and looking for two top notch people." Then, he lets it flow from there.

Sales Reps

This is Bob's idea, again. He suggests reps of all kinds: soda reps, liquor reps, hardware reps, computer reps, beauty supply reps, etc. These are the people who must go cold into stores and sell them on the products they represent. Many of them have excellent training from their companies, but are paid very little. Just go into a beauty parlor, or whatever, and say to the owner or manager, "Hi. My partner and I need two top sales people and we don't like to advertise. Of all the sales people, of all the reps you deal with, who's the best?" The owner will hand you the card of the best rep they have. Later, call this person. "Hi. I was in Junior's the other day and your name came up. The owner said he'd been in business for twelve years and never saw a better rep than you." (Always give a compliment.)

Then ask questions, "How did you get to be so good?" You might continue with, "It sounds like you're doing great, but I bet you're open for offers? Let's have lunch."

Classes and Seminars

Every so often, I collect free local newspapers, spread them out, and sift through them. I'm looking for classes, meetings, and other events that interest me (and even things that don't). Look for events geared toward people — people looking for businesses, or anything entrepreneurial. All these things attract me because the people who attend them are often perfect for MLM. I also read the daily papers, looking for the same things. Then I take my appointment book or calendar and mark in various happenings. For example, Tuesday, the second, at 7:30 p.m., there may be a ragtime piano player at the local coffee shop. Thursday afternoon, the women's club may be hosting a financial talk. Saturday night, there's a free lecture at the Back-Packers store on 9th St. I'll fill in the whole month this way. Then I get ready to have a good time.

A few weeks ago, I attended a tax seminar for business women. I showed up half an hour early, as I always do. This gives me time to "work the crowd." As soon as I pranced into the room, I checked out the ladies and began watching those coming in the door. I was friendly. I'd sidle close to one or she might, unsuspectingly, move toward me. With a big smile on my face I'd say, "Hi. What brings you here?" Then I'd listen.

To be polite, most people ask in return, "So, what brings *you* here?" If they don't ask, I tell them anyway, but I lose interest in them as prospects. When people aren't inquisitive about you, they probably aren't interested in people, and MLM is a people business. My answer for this particular class, with a look of wonderment on my face was: "I'm suddenly making so much money with my business that I *have* to find out about taxes!"

"Oh? What do you do?" is the expected response. I then tell them about my MLM business. But if they don't inquire, I mildly ask them, "What do you do?" And I listen closely. Do they like their work? Are they unhappy with it?

These are all clues for me. They help me know if they might be interested in something like MLM. Somehow, in some way, I manage to work the conversation around to what I do, or the products I have. Meanwhile, I'm just as chummy and unthreatening as a dog with no teeth.

Sales or Service People

I've also been known to shop a lot, singling out sales or service people who do especially good jobs. I'll say, "You have a great way with people and I like your feel. I'd love to have you working with me." Then, *sotto voce,* "Is this a job you want to be doing for the rest of your life? Give me your name and number."

Next I'll slip them the company magazine and whatever other product or company literature I have tucked away in my purse or pocket and say, "Read it. I'll call you in a few days." After that, I slink out of the store before the owner catches me. They don't want to lose their good people.

Advertise to Find Distributors

This works well for some people and is a thunderous dud for others. I cover advertising more thoroughly in Chapter Nine.

Trade Shows, Fairs, and Flea Markets

I've never cared much for these places. At fairs and trade shows, you have to talk too much. People eat, drink, or try on all your samples and stuff your expensive brochures in the trash as soon as they turn the corner. Prospects at shows are overloaded with hawkers' claims, products, flashing lights, and tall-tree stories. They have a great day, sampling and belching and looking for deals, then forget all about you as soon as they get home.

Flea markets and swap meet customers generally look for cheap stuff, and, most likely, your incredible products don't sell cheaply. They'll flare their nostrils at $19.95 and fly past you. However, some MLMers adore these places. The shows bring out the carnival personalities in such people. These are the people who love to talk and auction off prizes. When prospects leave their names and phone numbers, these kinds of people get a big kick out of calling five hundred people back in the next two weeks. That can make a carnival type feel as if they're really working. The law of numbers being what it is though; you have the same chance at finding "a good one" this way as you do anywhere else. So if you like it, do it.

Grocery Stores, Bank Lines, Gasoline Stations and Restaurants...

...and anyplace else your "victims" dare to show up. Multilevel makes you sociable. If you don't grin at people and start chatting, you don't get anywhere. Again, you just have to start talking. You can discuss the weather, the color of someone's shirt, or you can mention that their shoes are on the wrong feet. Anything that brings two people together and builds rapport, works. The idea is to use *every opportunity* to meet people, wherever you find them.

Other Ideas

Start asking people: "Who do you know that would like to make some extra money and could squeeze out six to ten hours a week to do it? Who do you know...who do you know? Who would you like to work with?"

Keep asking these questions of people you know or run into. If you ask, "Who do you know?" enough times, eventually some people will want to join you, or will recommend someone who will. Contact people in other MLMs. They probably won't listen to you, but you *can* keep in touch. If their company goes sour, they'll know about you.

Who from other MLMs have been after you? Tell those people, or anyone else you find, "My partner and I need one or two people who are great at recruiting." (Your partner

could be any of your upline, or downline.)
Joke with the people you're prospecting. Have a good time.

International Connections

At some point, your MLM may expand internationally, if it hasn't already. What can you do short of traipsing off to Egypt or Asia? Go to campuses and look for the nationality in question. Approach them, "Excuse me, are you French? If you are, I have a business opportunity you might like to hear about." Put notices on campus bulletin boards: "Attention: people with relatives or friends in Ireland. Are you looking for a fun job?" "Attention: people with relatives or friends in England. We have something that could make you money and get you a visit back home."

Check out Asian studies departments at universities, plus the Filipino/American groups, the Hispanics clubs, and so on. Go to embassies. Advertise in the countries in question.

Remember my trip to Singapore? It might have been less exciting, but more profitable to have researched the situation better and built a connection with someone there before I left.

Company Magazines and Other Literature

A word about company magazines: My current MLM company produces a beauty. By the time you've leafed through it, you're ready to sign up that instant. One of my downline, Peter, a big star in my group, uses the magazine to absurd perfection. He always carries a stack with him, along with product, in his car. A typical day for Peter goes like this:

"Excitin' news, Venus!" (Every day he leaves a message on my answer machine that begins with "Excitin' news! Call me right back!" I fall for it every time. Sometimes I even ask, "What? What's the exciting news?"

"What news?" he'll respond. That phrase is a habit he's developed to get people to return his calls promptly. It works every time with me, even after three years, and I know better.

"Excitin' news, Venus!" Peter yells, "I was in the grocery store today and here's this lady reading one of those scandal magazines. I rolled right up to her and said, 'You don't want to be reading that! It won't get you anywhere. Here — read this. You'll make tons of money selling this stuff, and you can stay home with your kids!' She followed me out to my car, Venus!"

He took a second to breathe, and continued, "I was eating lunch today with a friend at a big hotel. I said, 'Excuse me for a moment,' and took myself and my magazine to the washroom. So, I'm sitting in there, you know, and this man settles into the stall next to me. So, I go into my number. I'm noisily flipping the pages of our magazine and saying out loud, 'Oh my God, I don't believe this! This is *incredible*. I can't believe the money these people are making! And this stuff really works, too. Man, you've got to see this!' And I thrust the magazine under the stall. I'm waving it around, so of course the man takes it. By the time I'm leaving the washroom, he's clattering along behind me, holding his pants up and saying, 'Tell me more about this stuff!'"

Well, this works for Peter. I'm a bit more reserved, but I still get it out there. I also staple my card to the company magazine, and anything else that isn't either moving or breathing.

Maggie's Approach

Maggie is single, about thirty-eight, a mom, and determined to make this business work. Nothing deters her from her goals. (You want people just like Maggie!) A few weeks ago, she got some "free" tickets in the mail. These were $89.00 tickets to a business seminar lasting from 7:00 a.m. till 7:00 p.m.

What kind of business? We didn't have a clue, but decided it would be a great place for Maggie to "work the crowd."

Maggie's report to me went like this: "Well Venus, I got there real early, of course, and there were already about five hundred people in the audience. I was terribly excited because I could tell right away that these folks were all looking for a business to build. The first seminar leader talked for an hour and a half about buying property cheap and getting partners to help you. He didn't really say how to do it, because that was in all his tapes and books that he was selling. He went on and on about the amazing money to be made (which was nothing compared to our business!) and how these people needed to purchase his products right now!

"He was so amazingly good that by the time he reached the end of his talk, about three hundred people were rushing to the back of the room. They were pushing and kicking each other to be first with their credit cards and cash! I was stunned. These people were begging him to sell them stuff for $400 and $500. You could find the same thing at the library!

"Then the next speaker came on. He blustered on the same way, except this time he was hyping a different business, but it too was available on all his tapes, videos, and books for only $595.

"About this time, I started to get twitchy. I was scratching around in my seat and twisting my neck to look at all these anxious people. Some were sweating. They were desperate to hear the go-ahead to run to the back tables and buy! I was restless because I knew I had something better! And, not only that, mine only cost $35.00 to get involved. All these people should know about it! Soon, without planning it, I started mumbling. Little low grumblings were slipping out of my mouth.

"I've got something better," I'd whisper.

"Then, 'You're kidding? *That's* a good deal? Wish you could hear what *I've* got!'

"I was getting louder. People from five or six chairs in front of and around me were turning to look at me. That kind of encouraged me, I guess, because when the speaker said, 'Have you ever heard of a better deal?'

"I screamed, '*Yes!*' He ignored me and went on with his speech, building to a climax geared to promote a buying frenzy.

"'Who could pass up a deal like this one?!' he yelled.

"'I could!' I shouted.

"'There's no better opportunity available today!' he thundered.

"'I've got one! Over here!' I hollered.

"He gave up, I guess, and released the crowd to rush to the back of the room. Exhilarated, I hopped up on my chair and began waving my product around.

"Venus, because of that meeting, I got six distributors. And not just distributors. Good ones. People who were there looking for an opportunity."

The Probable Best Way
to Find Good Distributors

After much thought and checking through my best legs, I realized that the majority of good people I've signed came from *personal contact*. Most of them came to me as clients in my counseling business. Others came from reading my books. A few came from my previous MLM. My daughter introduced a few more. Two came from a friend. Each person I signed knew, liked, and trusted me. I believe that's the key. Some people that I signed dropped out, of course, but I count them because they signed good people downline.

So, if personal contact is the key, then it seems obvious that we need to meet more people. We must become more social. Join and go to places where people get to know us. Generally that takes a bit of time, which leads us, as I've mentioned before, to going to classes or teaching them, and becoming involved in clubs and community good works, projects, or service organizations. However, with the right personality, or practice, you can even develop this warmth with ads or cold calls.

I recently read an article about a man who does quite well recruiting over the phone, cold. He says it takes at least five calls to the same person. He sends MLM materials between calls. Eventually, he wins many of them over. How? He genuinely cares about them and becomes their friend. He identifies with their lives and situations. When they finally sign, they say it's because he's sincere, persistent, and seems to care about them.

Again, the key: They feel they know and trust him, because he's built a relationship with them. Some people can build that rapport in minutes. They may get lucky with someone they find on the street.

I think what we need most is to be very human and develop sincere relationships. It's simple — people are everywhere. But, where are the types that will appreciate and fit into your business? Identify those places and go there, join up, sign in, meet, advertise, call, contact...and become the friend with the *opportunity* that the person has been looking for all their life.

Approaching Potential Distributors
(Without Chasing Them Off)

People often ask me, "But once you've found a live person, how do you *really* start talking to them about your product or company?" My answer is that I *always* work it into the conversation. My approach is relaxed and simple. For example, perhaps a saleslady is helping me choose a dress. We chat a bit and then I'll say, "Do you like your work?" Or, "I need this dress for a party my company is giving in Madagascar." Either line opens the door to what I do for a living.

Sometimes when I'm standing next to a stranger and we're chatting about the weather, I just drop a pertinent statement or question into an otherwise vapid conversation. In my case, my business is health-related so I might ask, "Do weather changes cause you any physical problems?" After that question, I can hardly shut the person up, but when I do, I have a suggestion for them that informs them about my product(s).

Maybe you sell pots; still talking about the weather, you might say, "Did you ever catch rain in pots when you were a kid?"

Maggie uses this method a lot when she's at a function. If someone asks her, "What kind of work do you do?" She answers brightly, "Oh, I party for a living!"

"You what?" the person asks incredulously.

"I just come to things like this," Maggie says, "looking for people. I have a great time."

Quite often the person says, "Tell me all about it! I want to party, too!"

Other Ways

Awhile ago, I was signing papers to buy a house with my MLM earnings. The loan rep was obviously frazzled and stressed and needed one of my products. I just happened to have a bottle in my car, and so I sold it to her.

"Boy, you're really tensed up, aren't you?" I had asked. She had to agree that she was. I proceeded to tell her about the marvelous product I used to keep me calm. She thanked me profusely as she wrote out my check!

Four weeks later, I'm at the escrow company, signing papers. The girl in charge of me is gulping cokes and coughing mightily. I'm restraining myself because this selling business can get out of hand, but then her friend says, "How many cokes you want me to get you today, Freddi? A six-pack hold you?" And my lady says, "Gosh, at least. I need that caffeine!"

Well, I can't help myself. "I've got something in the car that gives energy without caffeine." I say. "I've been taking it for over a year and I love it." Then, I grin, because I know I look darn good, too. A little more chitchat and she has a bottle.

Now, I don't know if these two ladies will end up distributors but the potential is there. They both deal with the public and are workaholics. My chances are good. They could end up helping me pay for that house I just bought.

Maybe you sell multilevel life insurance; "I had an uncle, once," you could say, "and one day while he was standing in the rain he started sneezing, and then fell dead in the street. Didn't have any insurance, either, and that's why his wife and six kids had to come live with us. Changed my whole life. That's why I started selling life insurance. Do you have any?"

Perhaps you sell long distance phone service; "Boy, with this rain coming on," you'd gasp, "we'll be late getting home. Thank God, I've got the best phone system in the world. I can call my wife from this genuine 18-karat ruby ring here, on my pinkie finger!"

What I'm saying is, just slide over to a person, any-where, and be friendly. Work your business into the conver-sation. Be creative. Pretend you're a TV interviewer, or a talk-show host, out looking for talent and news stories. Drop your business or product line into the conversation. You can be gentle, just be sure to do it. *Nothing ventured...nothing gained.*

The Professional Approach

Professional MLM people have more professional advice. They suggest you nod discreetly and say, "I have a concept that might interest you. Do you have some time now to sit down and talk?"

If they don't (and this is Venus's advice taking over), I would say, "Give me your card." I never say, "May I have your card?" That gives them a chance to say "no!"

I also never say, "Here's my card." My friend, they will *never* call you. Do not hand out your card and go home and sit in hope. In this business you are the aggressor. Take their card and say, "I'll call you." Then, do.

Sometimes men say, "But, Venus, it's different for a man. You're a woman; people aren't afraid of you. They just hand their number over when you tell them to."

Men, if you are warm and friendly in a humane, non-sexual way, you can pull this off. I know it's a habit you may wish to keep, but you have to stop leering and lusting in your hearts. That's what makes you scary. Think business. Think of that houseboat on the Riviera that this business will get you. Talk about your dear, devoted wife, Elva, and your five darling little children. Scratch your leg and look harmless. Mention how much your dog loves you.

Subtle Approaches

Some people use this approach: They call their prospects and say, "I'm thinking of getting involved in this great business (or taking this new product), but I don't know much about it. Would you mind if a friend of mine (your sponsor, of course) calls you and tells you about it? Then, you can tell me what you think. I'd like your opinion." Likewise, help your distributor with this approach when he or she asks you.

Mary had an informal barbecue. She just told people it was a barbecue, but she also invited four sets of her upline. She fed all of them well, then let them loose on the crowd. They mixed and mingled and very casually mentioned, at every opportunity, the line of work they were in, or brought their products into the conversation. Then they just as casually mentioned that Mary was involved, too. I don't think anyone suspected they were at a business meeting. They had a great time and Mary now has some friends who are primed and ready for her products and business opportunity whenever she cares to drop the subject into a conversation.

The Honest Approach

You could also try the honest approach and say, "I'm having a spaghetti dinner at my house this Tuesday. Before we all get drunk, a friend of mine (again, your sponsor) is going to speak about an interesting opportunity. It won't take long, and afterwards we'll get down and have some fun. Can I count on you to be there?"

One lady fixes Mexican dinners. She does Mexican because it's cheap to make and most people will come out for food.

She'll say to a friend, "Hey, Harriet! I'm having a big Mexican do over here on Wednesday night. Lots of tamales, men, and beer. But, you have to listen to something to get supper. It'll be short, with a video and a sample of an interesting new dry skin scraper. You don't have to buy or sign anything, I just want you here. I figure if we're eating you'll come. You know how the two of us are (yuk, yuk)! I have to have your firm R.S.V.P. though, because I'm making batches of enchiladas and need a head count. Also, I have room for only a certain number of people. If you can't come, I'll ask somebody else." (Nobody likes to be replaced. Also, if you're up–front about what you're up to and make a joke out of it, you'll get people who'll come expecting to have a giggle, instead of feeling set-up.)

Get A Boat

Another couple I know owns a lovely boat. When they joined our group, they began having weekend boat parties. Each week, a new batch of friends drank and ate and partied while they learned all about the couple's new business. From each batch the couple would get a few distributors who would then invite a new cluster of prospects to the boat the following weekend. It kept expanding this way until the couple had a sizable downline. You may not have a boat, but what do you have, or what can you do, that gets people together?

If your sponsor is too far away to be physically there for you at a meeting, then consider having them call and talk to your prospects once you have them primed. If you're getting no help, or if your sponsor is a yo-yo, go farther upline for training. If it's not available, do it on your own. Don't let anything be an excuse for you.

How Not to Approach Distributors

There's a man I know who tries to sign *everybody* as a distributor. In airports, he plops down next to his victim, whips out his card, and starts his tape-recorded talk. On the plane, his seat partner is captive for the duration. And I'm warning you now, get out of his way when he goes shopping. I once saw him supporting and escorting an old, wispy, deaf lady to her car, haranguing her all the way about the benefits of working his MLM business. If you can still breathe, you qualify for his group. So run from him when he stops to get gas and don't sit near him in a restaurant. I've even seen him signing people at the gaming tables in Las Vegas.

The funniest moment came when our company was in Reno. At 2:00 a.m., I'm trudging back to my hotel room, and there's Lyle standing in the doorway of the gift shop. He flings his right arm parallel to the doorjamb and yells, "Congratulations on making the best decision you'll ever make! Your life will never be the same. I commend you."

I had to laugh, because it was 2:00 a.m., and while we were all having fun, Lyle was still hammering away at people. I also know that once Lyle signs someone, he rarely sees or talks to them again. He can't. He's off, signing new people. And he's a master at that. Occasionally, he gets lucky and signs a self-starter who jumps all obstacles and makes Lyle a little bit richer.

This works for Lyle; however, I do it differently. When I approach someone, I throw in a few questions like, "Are you happy in your job? Would you like to earn an extra $2,000 to $3,000 a month, and would you make time to do that?" I want to know, at least, if they are possible possibles...and if I could like them enough to work closely with them, and maybe spend the rest of my life in business with them. And, of course, if I do sign them, I work with and train them until they're either strong, or they expire.

Remember Lyle. Do not batter anyone or everyone about your company and products. If you start doing that, even your own kids will run from you.

Stan, a whiz in MLM, told me this story about a distributor he was coaching. "We were in a fancy department store when my man spotted a lady who worked there. He was just sure she was the type who should be in his downline. Before I could grab him, he went up to her and immediately started telling our whole company story. He hauled out all the brochures, samples, foldouts about the founding fathers, testimonials, amounts of money we make, his cousin's reactions; you know, did the whole damn dance.

"I finally pulled him away and rushed him to the car. I was sweaty and flushed as I said, 'Dick, Dick, Dick. No, no, no. She doesn't even know you. You know she works here. She's not going to run off tomorrow. What you should have done was ask her questions about herself and her life. Be a friend. When you walked away, she shouldn't have had any idea what business you're in. You could then come back. You could maneuver it so that you run into her again. The next time she would have had good feelings for you because you've already met and talked.' I explained to him that the process of approaching a new distributor is not selling. It's listening and asking questions. Don't throw your MLM business in people's faces."

Stan continued. "Dick, the second time you met that lady, after more questions, you could have given her a compliment. You could have said: 'You seem really good with people. Have you been looking around for other work? What are your career objectives? Do you make good money?...Well, give me a call when you're ready for a change ...' Then walk away. If she stops you, say, 'Let's go for coffee.' At coffee you ask more questions including, 'What do you know about network marketing/MLM?'"

Here's what cured me of pounding people and being obnoxious and overbearing about my multilevel.

At my old school friend, Fanny's, Christmas wedding dinner several years ago, about thirty of us had just settled around her aunt's huge oak table. A fire bounced and crackled in the fireplace. The Christmas tree was thick and sweetly hung with gingerbread boys and popcorn strings. Everyone was dressed up and behaving as we got ready to dip into and ladle out the Christmas meal. Just as I reached for the mashed potatoes, Fanny's cousin-in-law, Brad, 6' 5" and the human equivalent of a Butterball turkey, thundered, "You know what you all need here?!"

"What?" we all said in unison.

"This looks like a damn fatty meal to me," he said. We agreed. "And I guess you've noticed how much weight I've lost since Thanksgiving?" We looked, but we didn't notice. "Well," he boomed as spit gathered on his lower lip, "it's because I'm taking these pills! They're 100% natural, strained from beef bile! Guaranteed to absorb all the fat you eat!" He dramatically pulled a small bottle from his jacket pocket. "Only $24.65 a bottle," he said. "I'm selling these now. Let me tell you folks..." Brad slapped the bottle on the table and leaned forward. "This is a ground-floor opportunity! The best deal to hit this country since pancakes! This is the finest multilevel ever devised!"

I finished dishing out my mashed potatoes. Everyone else went about quickly filling their plates. Brad kept going, "This doctor at Stanford discovered this miracle cure for losing weight. Beef bile! That's it! Three every meal does the job. Thirty pills to a bottle. Here, I want you all to take these." Generously, he moved around the table, dropping three pills at each plate. Dutifully we swallowed them, although the dog got several. "Now," Brad bellowed, as he settled back into his seat, "I'm going to tell you the history of this product, the history of this company, and what it can do for you."

And he did. And he did. And he did. No one can over-talk Brad. It's a hopeless proposition to try. Emotionally chained to our chairs at the Christmas feast, we were battered and hounded unmercifully about his multilevel for an hour and a half.

At one point, I put my head in my hands; I was thinking of what I'd put my family and friends, and strangers through, with my enthusiasm about my multilevel. I leaned towards my mother and whispered. "I guess I deserve this." She laughed and agreed.

By the end of the meal, three things had happened: I had learned a good lesson, we were all quite annoyed and exhausted, and we all had terrible gas from those darn pills!

Don't Set People Up

Here's an example of how I once approached someone in a negative way. My daughter and I were buying a new car for her (more MLM earnings). The salesman was pleasant and very easy to deal with.

"Are you happy with your work?" I asked.

"Oh, pretty much so, I guess," he said. "I've been doing it for a year and a half."

I looked at him pensively and thought, "He likes to sell, but he's not delighted about car sales; however, he's been here a year and a half, so he sticks to something." I mentioned, between car talk, my products and opportunity.

Two hours later, a bit sweaty and frustrated, he asked if I'd give him my car business and buy that cute little red one for my darling daughter. I said I would, with one condition. He would come to my Tuesday night business meeting. "Is that part of the deal?" he asked.

"Yes."

"I'll be there," he said.

The ending of this story, which might have worked, was that he didn't show. He never came. Why? Because it was a set-up. I had him agree to something he obviously had no intention or interest in doing. He just wanted the sale.

I learned three things:

1. Never set somebody up.
2. Give them a choice.
3. He wasn't the kind of fellow who would have done well in my group anyway, because he didn't tell the truth or keep agreements.

I've included this story because it taught me a few things and may help you. On the positive side, it shows that you can use every opportunity to present your MLM. Just be creative.

Here Are a Few Things That Big MLM People Say Will Do You In When Approaching People

- Bad language and bad breath
- Being late
- Being too sexy; (If you're a woman, the wives will hate you, and the husbands will like you too much.)
- Smoking
- A dirty car
- Being poorly groomed (I didn't say poorly dressed; I said poorly groomed. Some people are impressed by business suits and some people are intimidated by them. Follow your own style. Just wipe the syrup off your pants.)

Those Other *Rotten* MLMs

Never argue the merit of or put down other MLM companies or products with prospects. Ask questions instead:

"Why did you join that MLM?" (Or "Why did you get out?")

"What did you, or do you, like and hate about it?

"You got in to make money, right?"

If the person is still in a particular group, notice if they're disgruntled or mindlessly hyped. Once you know their answers, they're helpless before you. They're helpless, that is, if you are truly in a better MLM. If so, you can confidently say, "I'll show you what I'm doing...and you show me what you're doing." Just remember, if you're in a good company, the other MLMs are just training and sifting people for your group. Stand by, watch, and wait.

Sincerity Wins

It doesn't matter what you're selling, you're not selling — you're teaching. You believe in the products you're promoting, right? You'd better, because if you don't, the people you approach won't believe in them either.

I generally sell health in some form, because I believe in it (just as you need to admire, respect, and even love your products). I'm obsessed with health, I'm neurotic, and I'm a hypochondriac. This makes it easy for me to be continually excited (in varying degrees) about my product. When I'm telling (teaching) someone about my product, there's not a lie or a wishy-washy thought in my head about it. I want you to feel good, to be happy and healthy. I'm not thinking, "Gee, I've got fifteen boxes of this stuff in the garage that I have to unload!"

One day, I asked Summer why she thinks I do so well

with this current business, because I couldn't figure it out. She pondered a bit, then said, "You're always so enthusiastic about it, Mom. A few people get rattled by you and think your products have got to be too good to be true, and it scares them off. But everyone else gets electrified by your sincerity and ends up buying stuff or signing up."

I think she's right. I tell these people, my friends (and that's how I feel about everyone unless they prove otherwise), everything I know about my product's background, uses, and results. I either show company videos on the spot, send them home with one (or an audio), or mail them out for review. I answer every question, even if it's with an "I don't know."

If someone says, "I have to think about it," I sincerely ask, "What do you need to think about?" Maybe I've already thought about the same thing. I try not to be pushy and overbearing. Usually, after I've unloaded all my facts and enthusiasm, I say, "But, you decide. Only do it if it feels right for you. You have to make your own decisions and live your own life. I only want you to use my products or be my partner in this business if you're going to be happy with what you're doing."

How to Set Appointments with Prospects

After finding and approaching people, you need to get them to listen to you.

To set appointments with prospects to get them to sign up, buy your products, and work the business, the person must buy *you*, first.

Selling Yourself

Be honest:
- How well do people like you?
- How much influence do you have with them?
- Do they respect and trust you?

While you're revamping your character, you might need to have your upline help you with some people.

How about your downline? Is there a distributor who needs you to step in and talk to a person with whom they have little credibility? That person may be your downline's friend or family member. You're a stranger, so they assume you must know something, but, of course, their kid or cousin doesn't have the brains to know how to chew peanut butter.

Many people think they need to set appointments with people to introduce them to MLM. I rarely do that, but I'll teach you how. (Once you know the basics, you can do it *your* way, too.) What do I mean when I say I rarely make "real" appointments?

When you say, "Let's meet for coffee and I'll present my program," or, "How about if I come over about 7:00 p.m. tonight to show you the setup." That's exactly how most people will feel — set-up, mad, and resistant, especially if you drag along your wheeler–dealer upline. Now, I know this may work for some people, and it's a tried and true method, but I just don't like it. I simply prefer to "Do 'em where I find 'em." I'm so casual about my presentations that people rarely know they're being presented.

When I meet a prospect, I just casually mention a few things about my product that's appropriate for their situation. I might whip out a youthful picture of my company's old founding father. Maybe I'll pull a bent sample out of my purse. Nothing looks staged or planned. I get the person's card. I tell them I'll call them back. I remark on the stiff wind that's blowing today and that it's a good thing that the hair on our heads is real, or some other such congenial nonbusiness remark.

Following Up

If you've met someone, taken their card, and promised to call them, then you're going to have to do what you promised.

When you get home, call. Or, give your nerves a chance to settle down by sending them a company brochure and a short note: "I promised I'd call you, and I will in a few days." Then, call them.

Once again, the *professionals* say, "Never tell people what your business is, exactly. Get the appointment." That works for them, but it doesn't for me.

I say on the phone, "Hi. This is Venus. I met you at such and such and you gave me your card." (Remind them who you are, even if this takes five minutes and you're down to describing the lace on the slip that hung outside your skirt. No matter how handsome and charming you feel, chances are the person won't remember you.)

"How did you like the sample I gave you?" you might ask, or, "We didn't have much time to talk yesterday. Could you tell me more about your swollen toes?" (Your product just happens to help swollen toes.) You could say, "You mentioned that your husband is out of work. That must be tough. When my husband was laid off, awhile back, I got involved in this wonderful business. Now he doesn't care if they ever want him back! We don't need the money!" (Your multilevel would fill their income gap, nicely.)

From there, tell them to come on over and pick up some "Swollen Toe Juice", or come watch a short videotape, and bring their husband before he gets lazy!

If you're advertising for people, the following idea also works for folks who call on your ads. I tell the people what product I represent and why it should interest them. I tell them we need to meet and that I'll show them a short video and give them samples of the product. I tell them we can look each other over and see if we'd like to work together. I say, "There's no pressure here, because I'm only looking for a few good people. This is not a boiler room operation. I'm going to spend a lot of time with the people I choose." I make it clear that they are not interviewing me as much as I am interviewing them. I am casual and personable, just as though I'm talking to a friend.

"Can you come over tomorrow? How about noon? Or would one o'clock be better?" (The professionals would say you should meet them at a coffee shop, you should go to them, or have them come to your office. *I* make them come to me. It's less wear on my body and time, and doesn't seem to affect my income!) We set a date and time. I set it soon, before they lose interest or their family gets to them. ("Oh for God's sake, Gus! Are you actually going to get hooked into another multilevel ripoff? You've still got twenty cases of Poobah Juice in the garage from the last scam. You silly fool!") Often, I'll book several or more people at one time and hope that at least one keeps the appointment.

How to Physically Sign Someone

Let's say that you're calling people about your business and products, even though you shake like jelly when you do. You finally get them to a home meeting, or coffee, or you just talk to them where you find them. You're making lists and giving samples and doing everything right, but you're hysterical. You're hysterical because you can't seem to sign anyone.

Here's a good method for signing when you're talking with one person. I just happen to have a distributor kit close by and drag it over. "Look," I say as I rip the box open, "let me just show you what's in our kit." Then I quickly pull out a few relevant pieces, let them look for two seconds, and then toss the stuff aside. What I'm going after is the distributor application form. I yank it out with a grand gesture and put it in their lap. "Look," I point, "here's where I fill out my part. And here," I say dramatically, "is where you sign." I hand them a pen and ask, "What do you want to do?" Well, I find out. They do or they don't. If they don't, I just tape up the kit and move on. If they do, they take the pen and sign. To hurry their decision I often say, "You might as well. A lot of people sign up so they can get the products cheaper. They order a case and sell the rest to their friends. That way it pays for their habit." Most people think that's a grand idea.

This last sentence works well in a home meeting or over the phone. Just say they can get it cheaper and that they can get their friends to support their habit. I'm not saying that these people will be great distributors, but at least you'll have signed someone and you'll feel better.

Complications

Should you place your distributors under other distributors? Some people say yes; you can help build your downline by putting people under them. However, I rarely do this. I only do it with great caution, as it's almost like an arranged marriage. The two people need to meet to see if they're compatible first. Sometimes the person whom you're signing will feel outraged or hurt because they wanted to be with you, not someone else.

It can be a splendid marriage...or one fraught with

disharmony or disinterest. Also, your distributors are more likely to get lazy and demanding, expecting you to build more and more of their business for them. Frankly, it's much better to help distributors find people from their own circles.

Choosing the Right People for Your MLM Group

Who to Choose

Choosing the right people for your MLM group may be the most important issue of your whole campaign. After much observation of my group and others, I feel this comes even before hard work and persistence

The people who receive the biggest checks in MLM have signed distributors under them who are hard workers and who also earn big checks. Sometimes these people are old-time MLMers (meaning they've been involved in multilevel for years) and people with sales experience. But what if you don't know or can't shake current or former MLMers or sales people into joining your group? Although you may be tired of signing bellhops, waitresses, busboys, car mechanics, and housewives, there's nothing wrong with these types. If they have a real need to succeed and a burning desire to make it, regular people can be the best! I love it when someone tells me, "I have to make it in this business!" The problem comes when you realize that most of these folks are starting just where you are in MLM and sales: ground zero. They know only a little bit less than you do. And again, on the average, it's going to take some time (maybe a long time) to get you all through MLM college. While that's happening, maybe you'd like a few faster runners in the group.

The Ideal Types of Distributors

- People who may have had past MLM experiences but aren't totally ruined by them!
- People who have been helped, healed, dazzled, or impressed by your products.
- Women. Many MLMers are women. They gravitate to a profession where they can make as much, or more, money than men. Lately, more women are wishing to leave the stresses of the corporate world and work from home.
- Self-starters. People who are able to work well on their own.
- People who absolutely want this business to work, recognize the opportunity, and seriously commit to working the business.
- Steady hard-workers with positive outlooks, who are open-minded and happy.
- People who want more out of life. Maybe they have a camper but want a motor home. Maybe they have a functional tan car, but want a red Mercedes.
- People who want freedom, flexibility, and mobility. Look for people who have social contacts and control over their own lives. These might be insurance or real estate people, because they choose those lines of work for the above-mentioned reasons. These kinds of people must also initiate to find business. They can't

sit back and wait for it to come to them.
- Recruiters. These are folks who have seemingly snatched people out of thin air and built something.
- Teachers. They know how to teach and manage people and their pay is usually abysmal.

Ideal Qualities in Prospective Distributors

According to MLM *authorities*, people who are successful in MLM have certain characteristics:
- They take calculated risks and make decisions.
- When there are problems, they don't wail and blame — they solve them.
- They have healthy self-images, generally thrive on competition, and have a goal or goals they strive for.
- They are often creative, persistent, and they complete projects.
- They are people-lovers.

Examples of Qualities That Succeed

Today, one of my downline, Sharon, said, "When I was in another multilevel, they told us: 'Don't put much hope in the people who flash in and do tremendous volume. They rarely last because their habit is to triumph and then go on to other things. Look for the people who come in slowly and build slowly, with depth and strength. They are the ones who stay.'"

The following examples from my downline may help you identify and use the inborn talents of others that will lead to your, and their, success. Identify the talent in all the numbers. Once you find these kinds of people, you have something to build on:

Deah: I call her The Mother of Bakersfield. She's been with me for about two years and has weathered many a depression while building her business. Deah, surely, slowly, and consistently, has labored to build a good group. It's been a lot like being pregnant. Some days you just want to get out of the deal, but the thing keeps growing, even though day by day you can't see it.

At this point, almost everyone in Bakersfield is somehow under Deah in our multilevel. And she's good to them, watching out for them and helping where needed, just like a good mom does.

That's why she's The Mother of Bakersfield. Deah was born with staying power, a loving attitude, and persistence. These qualities, repeated over and over, keep taking her closer to the top.

Belinda: Belinda carries a big bottle of her product under her arm wherever she goes. It's so odd-looking that people often ask her what it is. She had been wanting to contact some people from a particular company for a long time.

One day, as she was pacing up and down in front of their offices wondering how she could approach them, a thought struck her. With the bottle firmly planted under her armpit, she trotted into the building. Standing in front of the receptionist's desk, she put on a puzzled face. Then, looking around, she did a good job of appearing confused. The woman behind the desk asked if she could help

"Is this an insurance office?" Belinda innocently asked.

"No," the woman replied. "Who are you looking for?"

Startled, Belinda quickly blurted a made-up man's name. Fortunately the woman didn't know him, but she did ask, "What's that weird bottle under your arm?"

Of course, Belinda sold her the bottle, and had her *in* with that company.

Look for people like Belinda who are willing to take risks and be creative.

Noelia: Noelia prays. She's an *Angel Connector*. From what she's told me, she has a natural faith in higher powers and hikes hand in hand with God. Through use she's acquired a clearer channel than most of us.

Awhile back, Deah called me. We had a meeting set up. I was going to drive for five to six hours in the scorching middle of summer to Baked— Bakersfield to do a business meeting for her and Noelia, her downline. Now, Deah was snuffling into the phone, "I'm so depressed, Venus. I've advertised and put out flyers and called everyone I know, and I don't think anyone's coming to our meeting."

"Listen, Deah," I said firmly, "I've set time aside for this. I'm driving a long way for this. You'd better have a big crowd there! That's it. I'll see you tomorrow."

The meeting was standing room only. Every chair was filled, and people lined the walls of the clubhouse. "So why all the tears and depression?" I asked. "You had a phenomenal turn-out." Deah and Noelia glanced at each other, looked a little sheepish and grinned.

"Well," Noelia said, sort of snorting into her hands, "you know how I like to pray about things? About an hour before the meeting, we were feeling desperate, so I hauled Deah in here and we prayed over every chair! We prayed that there would be a rear-end in every chair, Venus! Then we went around the whole room and prayed some more. And you don't know this, Deah, but after we finished and you went to get the punch, I ran in here and prayed some more!"

Noelia used a natural ability and added hard work to it. She's become a genius at touching the other side, and this brings her success.

Peter: Peter was born excited, and the excitement has never flagged. He's one of fifteen children who were all born to hustle. After two and one-half years, he's still excited about our products and the marketing plan. He still sees the gold in every person and every presentation. Peter is also our *Dream Spinner.*

One day he said to me, "Venus, whenever I talk to a person, I paint word pictures of their future success!" He does this with me, too. "Venus!" he'll shout, "By this time next year...you'll be making $80,000 to $100,000 a month. And I'll have passed you! I can see you now, with a resort home in the mountains and $600,000 in the bank. Oh, I tell ya Venus, it's happenin'!"

He means it, too. Peter was born with a brash and optimistic nature. When you're with Peter, you believe anything he says, you sign up, and soon you're building that big business he's painted. Peter has used these abilities to survive, and now that he's perfected them, they're paying off in a different way. His business is flourishing.

Rochelle. This is a little side story about a lady who isn't in my group, but I wish she were! I went to school with her from the first grade to adulthood. Afterwards, for at least twenty years, I dreamed about her. We had been friends, but not best friends, so there was no logical reason for her to keep intruding in my night life. It used to bother me. There was Rochelle, *again,* last night. Why?

All through school she had been an over-achiever. She certainly wasn't the brightest person, or the prettiest, but she got the best grades, was a cheerleader, student body president, got the most recognition and awards, and was active in sports. She seemed to be without any inborn talent or excessive brains, but she did better than any of us, at *everything.*

Several years ago, I stopped dreaming about her. That was it; she was gone. I was wondering why one day, when, pop! The answer came to me. I had become *successful.* Rochelle had been the rabbit in front of the greyhound all those years; and it was I who was running to win. Now I didn't need her example anymore. I was (am) an over-achiever too, I realized. I just hadn't recognized or used the ability before. Apparently my subconscious had, and had used Rochelle to inspire me.

You can help yourself by looking for over-achievers like Rochelle.

Sylvia: I contacted Sylvia in the first month that I started my business. Five months later, I was still calling, to tell her the latest stories about my products. Finally, I took her to lunch.

Once there, I was alternately charming and sulky. I liked her a lot, but she'd never watched my presentation videos. She had managed to lose them. She couldn't find the informative books that I had sent her, and, frankly, didn't care a twit.

However, after that lunch she felt so guilty that she tried the product. Three days later, completely sold on the stuff, she joined me. She's now one of my best downline.

(This is actually a story about *my* qualities as a distributor. *I never give up.* If I know someone will be good, I keep after them, in a pleasant way, of course. We're all here to live our own lives and make our own choices; I just stand hopefully by and grin at those I hope will choose *my* way.)

Special Types
AKA: Dysfunctionals

As mentioned earlier, there are certain accepted qualities to look for in distributors. However, the authorities have neglected to mention something that only Venus, it seems, would dare to do. What I call "bent" or "dysfunctional" personalities seem to do exceptionally well in MLM. We're the people who come from dysfunctional backgrounds, often being Adult Children of Alcoholics (ACA's), or come from other abusive or odd families. Dysfunctionals are those of us who are driven, compulsive, obsessive, hysteric, recovering alcoholics, recovering drug addicts, recovering sex addicts, etc.

Rescuers would fall into this lumpy group, too. We're the ones who want to save the world through good works, and this includes saving people financially with a good multilevel business. We generally like crises and excitement, and MLM certainly provides this for us.

Gamblers also fall into the dysfunctional group. All of us are waiting for the ace in the deck, the big spin, or the winning number. MLM provides this thrill. We're always just one person away from becoming a millionaire. Pick the right distributor and you're set for life. MLM gives you better odds, too. Once, I bought my dad fifty lotto tickets. He loves lotto. I felt sure that with fifty tickets something exciting would happen. It didn't. He made $2.00. I thought, "*Shoot!* If I'd talked to fifty people about my business, I would have made a lot more money!"

Dysfunctionals often need to succeed at all costs, and MLM gives us the arena in which to do it. We're enterprising and persistent. We delight in channeling all our energies into work. Often we're a bit *ticky* in the way we do it, though. For example, when someone tells me that I won't succeed or laughs at my dreams, I think, "Watch me, buddy." For whatever unhealthy reason, I thrive on succeeding against all odds and dire prophecies. I get a huge bang out of people thinking I'm just a regular, ditzy woman — a woman who wears jeans and works out of her kitchen, a lady with plenty of charm, but not much sense. Then I proceed to outperform most executives by making a fortune right in front of their eyes. It makes me happy, you know?

Revenge

Sometimes revenge works well for me too. One of my sisters has a talent for making me feel inferior because she's so bright. Through the years, every time I've mentioned my hobbies — herbs, health, alternative medicine, or MLM — she is critical. She, being from a medical and more orthodox business background, feels equipped to tell me that I'm misinformed about my field or venture. Her husband, Dick-the-Doctor, has spent years telling me that he worries about me being jailed for my unorthodox beliefs and practices. Living the *approved life* has brought them a huge "Dallas"-type home on rolling woodlands. They have a studio-barn the size of our parents' home, a black-bottomed pool, spa, a motor home the size of Nantucket, and every plaything you can imagine.

Periodically, as I built my current business, I'd ask my sister, "How much does Dick make a month, now?" In my mind I'd say, "OK, when I've passed you up by a good $5,000 a month, I'll just slip my success into the conversation." That goal of sweet revenge helped me to build this business. It kept me going through the hard times.

I'm quite aware that I'm a nut, and that revenge isn't the nicest quality, but I use these quirks to my advantage. Rather than cry and complain about my background and resultant patterns, I use them in positive ways, while I'm getting them therapied out of my psyche. I've become successful. You might look for more people like me. You can probably find most of us in analyst's offices or ACA meetings.

I *am* serious about this theory. People who have things to prove and needs to fill do well in MLM. We're often pretty obsessive about things, so we stick with MLM, and this works to our advantage because we feel compelled to succeed.

Caution!

One cautionary note, however. The folks who are still wrapped up in blaming, complaining, and heavy practicing of their addictions are not ready. You want those who are moving, or have moved, beyond that out-of-control stage that's filled with self-pity.

One last thought. Be sure to channel all your neuroses, too. Put them into something that makes you money. I used to specialize in exciting, emotionally shattering romances, but I gave them up. With MLM I can suffer all I want, and it pays better.

Gray-haired Marvels

I've noticed the preponderance of older gray-haired people in my company and I've wondered why and where they came from. Of course, my product offers a health benefit, but I feel there's another reason they're involved and doing so well: these people have *life* behind them. They know a lot, and they know how to do a lot. Maybe they were retired and found it cloying and boring. Maybe they needed the money. Maybe my company came into their lives, picked them up and danced them around like a tumbleweed. Maybe MLM carried them off to Kansas and the *magic* made their lives worth living, not to mention the lives of their lucky uplines!

How do you find these people? They're probably not in those retirement communities built by the River Styx, where people wait for death, right across the street from the fast food restaurant and the mortuary.

Consider the AARP (American Association for Retired People). The association accepts people age fifty and over, when there's still plenty of kick left! Get a copy of their magazine, *Modern Maturity*. You might want to put an ad in it. Better yet, get a copy of one of those free magazines for seniors. You can usually find them in the library. Try putting an ad in one of them. It's a local publication and should draw people close by. Try senior centers — put an ad on their bulletin board or volunteer your time to help out. There are many capable people who would love to augment their social security. Many of these people built their financial freedom and closed shop early so they could direct their own lives. Now, they've seen the world, lunched till they're bloated, need more money, and are ready to build again.

Think about other ways you can tap this venerable and knowledgeable market.

Entrepreneurial Types

When I was about seven, I leafed through a magazine, found, and ordered, on my own, one hundred boxes of Christmas cards from the *Cheery Card Company.* The company actually sent them! I piled those cheery cards into my little red wagon and trudged out to do business. My neighborhood consisted of a house about every mile or so, so it took awhile. I remember dragging that wagon up dusty rutted roads to the farmers' homes. All their dogs would come roaring out to greet and escort me. "Creak, creak, creak," my old wagon's racket and the yelping dogs would bring out the farmer's wife. I'd get a glass of juice and maybe unload one box of cards.

Within a week I was out of houses, but I still had ninety boxes of Christmas cards. My dad had to buy them.

Later, as I've mentioned, I went into the paper doll business. I'd draw paper dolls for my little school mates and sell them for three cents a piece. That was the exact change from their ice-cream money. By selling three sets of dolls, I could buy ice cream with two cents left over.

I suppose this kind of thing runs in families. When my daughter was seven, she began making jewelry and selling it to her schoolmates. She was so successful that her grammar school had to make a new rule: NO SELLING ON THE SCHOOL GROUNDS.

Apparently Summer was so aggressive with her wares that she was getting all the children's lunch money. She was causing children to be late to class, and fights were erupting over favorite jewelry pieces. However, the new "no selling" rule on campus didn't stop Summer. Each morning she'd calmly bundle up her handmade jewelry and set off for school a bit early. She was right there at the crosswalk each morning, barely off the school grounds, doing business as the kids came to class. After school, she'd run out to the same spot and promote more frenzied buying.

Keep an eye on these enterprising kids. You'll want to nab them when they're old enough. In the meantime, start asking grown kids, "Did you ever have a lemonade stand? Shine shoes? Play on the ball team, sell candy bars?" Even though they're older and heavier, they still have those little enterprising, entrepreneurial hearts

Learning To Discriminate

Your distributors come from the list of prospects that you continually and painfully put together and carefully court. In the beginning you may be grateful for anyone who can breathe and say "Yes, I'll sign up." Later, you will cry fretfully about the sluggish downline you're trying to whip along, while you wonder what's wrong.

Most likely the problem lies within all the people whom you've signed in your indiscriminate frenzy. Now that you've learned where to look for people, ideal qualities, general types, and approaches, it's time to narrow things down.

Be Selective

On one particular evening I was half an hour early to a function. You know, one of those places I go to scout for business. I managed to talk to four ladies. Three were totally worthless for my purposes. I did, however, find them entertaining. One woman was a secretary and single mother. "I hate my work," she said, "but it's safe and secure and I'm never going to leave. I'd never take a chance on something else. I know I'll never make more than $20,000 a year."

I knew right off that I didn't want to spend my time building up her self-image and baby-sitting her. The other two were simply dead in life. I moved on.

The fourth lady was pleasant. I liked her right off. We chatted about her work and (surprise!) a bit about mine. Spontaneously (ha!), I rummaged around in my purse and dragged out a rumpled sample of one of my products. As I handed it to her with a laugh (and a brochure) I said, "Give me your name and phone number. I'll call you tomorrow and see how you liked this stuff." She ended up buying two of my products that night (of course, I had them in my car) and more within the week.

After talking to her several more times by phone, I said, "So why don't you come to a meeting with me? You're not crazy about your job, you love our products and we like each other, so let's check it out." She did, and signed up with me that night.

This story is only semi-ended. The rest of the tale starts from here. I need to get her to more meetings, she needs to be trained, she needs to make a commitment, and she needs to get to work. She may last...and she may not. She may join the scores of people who fade away, or become one of the few who changes her entire life, positively, for the rest of her life through MLM. The point of this story is, however, that I selectively chose her. As "charming" as I was, I could probably have signed the other three ladies, but why? I'd have had three dead distributors to pummel and drag around. All four were adventurous enough to take a class, so they must have had *some* qualities we've previously discussed as ideal. But, each of the remaining three didn't have *enough* of what it takes and I quickly saw that. I'd learned to discriminate. You will, too. It takes time and a lot of practice, but you'll improve. Here are a few ideas to make it easier.

Sort People into Piles

Ask a person you've just met, "Would you like to double your income in the next twelve months? Do you have some extra time?" Or, "could you find an extra twelve to fifteen hours a week in order to earn $100,000?" If they say no, then let them do their own thing and spend your time on someone else. There are two hundred fifty million people in this country — don't waste your time with those who aren't serious about your opportunity.

The following is not an original thought of mine. I picked it up somewhere: "Remember this about people. Some you thought *would,* won't. Some you thought *could,* don't. The ones you *want to,* can't. It settles down to: *some will, some won't — so what.*"

Think about this when you're sorting people.

Sometimes Discrimination is Not Easy

Here are a few loose ideas about learning to recognize the jewels (and the stones).

When Jeri Ann signed, I figured she was a jewel. She

loved the product. She had grown weary of nursing and wanted out. She also wanted to kick her abusive boyfriend out of the house, but she didn't have the money to survive alone. She wanted to live her own life, dependent on no one. She had compelling reasons to make her new business work. So she began to work...hard. Feeling confident, she booted her boyfriend out.

"Hurrah," I encouraged her. "You're on your way to financial freedom."

Then she got a slew of no's from people. Next, she started to whine and complain about the company. Then I didn't hear from her. Eventually, I heard that she'd met another man, was engaged to him and had quickly and quietly dropped her high ambitions. I'd judged her too quickly; I had believed that she was ready to follow through on plans for her own life.

Then there was Neal. He was a massage teacher, a vegetarian, took herbs and vitamins, meditated, practiced nonviolence and chastity, and communed with the moon. He had always felt that money was unnecessary and a bit dirty. Then, at thirty-five, he realized that if he had to massage and scrimp till he died, he'd die a lot faster. His body was beginning to complain with the rigors of his profession. When he found an MLM company and product he believed in being pushed under his nose, the "real" Neal stepped out. A born businessman woke up and took over. How did I know this might happen? He is well versed in health products, believes in the company, and his job was killing him. He also has a sister who is a big name in another MLM. I suspected it might run in the family. Look for people who can see an opportunity, like to work hard, and have good reasons to do so! Some of these people will hang around long enough to succeed — because they have to!

What About Those People You Already Have?

Since people die and revive quite often in this business, perhaps the best advice I can give is to observe your dormant people carefully. When the faintest heartbeat sounds, run in with the jumper cables. If after repeated attempts they don't revive, or keep relapsing, let them go. Perhaps their Greater Reward lies elsewhere.

Who to Help, Who to Let Go

Reba was letting her business droop. She'd started off with plenty of enthusiasm, but, when the inevitable bumps hit her a bit too hard, she lagged.

"OK," I said, "what's going on? I haven't heard from or seen you in quite awhile."

"Well," she answered, "we moved, and now it's Halloween, and the kids have birthdays coming up."

"Your sponsor called me," I said, "and told me that she put someone under you and you haven't contacted them."

"Yes," Reba whined, "I just haven't had the time."

"I can understand that," I said. "If you decide you ever want to do the business again, let us know."

I'm not unfeeling or cruel. It's taken me years to learn that I have limited time. Now, I work with those who *want* to do the business and *prove* to me that they do. They prove that by calling me, going to meetings, giving meetings, and *doing* what needs to be done. If someone sincerely wants to make it, I'll work with them until we either win or both tip over trying.

Sometimes it's hard to know who to work with, or how much. One woman in my group bought eleven cases of product, then stopped working when she was just one case short of becoming a manager.

Periodically she revives, pulls the straw out of her hair,

and says, "Now, I'm really getting serious this time!" She buys a few more cases, and disappears again.

I worked on another lady, Carol, for five months. Finally, she signed into the business, but she still wouldn't do anything. I knew she could be sensational, so I kept after her. I waited through her trip to India. I waited until her daughter left for college. I waited until her husband was out of work. I waited until I had worn her down. She's now one of my best people. You just never know. Be careful about prejudging people. Their circumstances change.

All this, of course, leaves you wondering, "So how *do* you tell the difference between a Reba and a Carol?"

Realize that Reba *said* she wanted to build a business, but her actions showed me otherwise. She made a lot of promises that she rarely kept. Carol, on the other hand, never said she wanted to do the business. In fact, she begged me to leave her alone. But I knew that she could be successful — and would be successful in this business — so I kept after her.

If, after she'd signed *and* committed, she didn't follow through, I'd have eventually dropped her, too. If you have a gut feeling about a person, follow it, either way.

Blind Luck

Sometimes blind luck factors in. I signed a lady out of state named Anne. For over a year, I called her once or twice a month and sent her my newsletters. She never returned my calls or made any comment. I knew she could, and should do the business, so I never paid any attention to her silence. It never entered my mind that she might be totally uninterested in building a business. I thought she was just slow. After about a year and a half, she perked up and started to work. Two and a half years from the time I signed her, I went to Texas to give a meeting for her huge group. Imagine my shock when she introduced me to the bunch by saying, "This is the lady who kept calling me every month and sending me things — when I wasn't the least bit interested. My husband and I kept saying, 'When is Venus going to get a clue?' "

Your Character

Something needs to be said about your character. When you're looking for people to place in your downline, if you're not aware, you're going to attract, find, and approach people just like you! Think of the people you have in your group right now. Kind of a shocker, huh? After careful thought and observation, I realized I have a tendency to live in Fantasy Land. I go about thinking that everyone is honorable and just and fair....like me! Then I get a distributor who *borrows* product or money from me and I never see it or them, again.

"Why me?" I used to wail. Because I didn't see them clearly, as they really were, that's why. But, they saw me for the sucker I was, and were quite attracted.

Hope Won't Do It

A lady in my downline finally realized her group wasn't doing well because she lived in the Land of Hope. And, so did all the people she attracted to her, whom she choose to have in her downline.

"I hope this will work out," she'd say, or, "Hopefully, he'll be a good one," or, "I'm hoping hard."

Eventually, she got a little therapy and started her whole business over with new people...and without quite so much hope.

Another man, George, had it pointed out to him that he

was confused (couldn't see it himself, of course) and was advised to take on a clear-headed partner.

Look over your downline people again (or those you "hope" to have in your downline). Now, what's *your* personal problem? It's time to fix it if you want to insure your personal happiness and financial success.

Yes, MLM is much, much more than just a business.

Seeing Through Your Preconceptions

What kind of people do you want in your group?
• Honest?
• Hard-working?
• Dependable?
• High-minded?

You will have to see clearly to choose these people. Here's a way to do that: Imagine that your head is full of beliefs. It's stuffed full of ideas and thoughts about people, life, and the world. They are those ideas that society and other people put on you which color your outlook.

Remember how my beliefs told me that everyone was just and moral and would act honorably? My eyes were seeing through a carnival of illusion. Those sweet little ideas made me feel good, until I got scalped at the ring-toss. I then realized that those comfortable beliefs were in the way, and I couldn't see what really was. Make sure that you consciously recognize all of your preconceptions about people. It will save you a lot of grief.

Eventually, in order to see through my preconceptions more easily, I began to imagine that the *I*, or, conscious part of me, rose above my head and was able to *clearly* look at people. Although I felt foolish at first, I began to notice that by doing this I was actually able to see the lizards I was looking at — and boy, there were a few! I found I could then say, "Nice to meet you, nice to have known you, better I know you no more!" and move on. I didn't want them in my MLM group...or my life.

Getting Over Negative Beliefs About Selling

Dee Ann and I were having lunch yesterday. She represents a lot of people when she snuffles , "I've heard what you've said about finding people, but I've talked to everyone I know and everyone I don't know, and there are just no more people to talk to!"

Step Outside Your Circle

"Step outside your circle!" I shouted. MLM teaches us to be friendly, to extend ourselves. There are millions of people in the world. How can we possibly think we've exhausted our supply of contacts? Some suggestions:

- Try shopping at the same stores. Learn the names and lives of the salespeople.
- Go to the same gas station and pretend the owner is your Uncle Jim.
- Choose a few restaurants and frequent them until you feel that the owner and service people are family, and they feel the same about you.

"Pretty soon," I told Dee Ann, "you'll find that your neighborhood is full of friendly relatives, and you will become more happy and secure in your life. As a bonus, most of these people are sales oriented, and wouldn't they be great with your product? Tell them about it."

"Probably someone else has already talked to them," Dee Ann hedged.

"For God's sake, Dee Ann!" I said, exasperated. "The world is loaded with people. Look!" I jumped up and trotted to the restaurant window. "Come here! There goes one now! And another! Look, there's two in that blue car. And three in that yellow one!"

"OK," Dee Ann admitted, "there are lots of people."

"Next," I said, "you have to *believe* in whatever you're sharing with people. I believe that the products I promote are here to serve humankind, and I feel it's my job to teach people about them. If I don't even *tell* them about them, how can they make a decision one way or the other? I'm cheating people if I let it go unsaid." (And you need to feel the same way about the excellent herbs you sell, or cosmetics, water distillers, or two-sided toothbrushes.)

"Well, I'm shy," Dee Ann protested. "I feel like I'm bothering someone when I tell them about my product or business."

I think I surprised Dee Ann when I answered, "Maybe you're just self-involved?"

Selling is Sharing and Caring About the Other Person

You're self-involved if you're more concerned about *your* feelings being hurt if you get a "no" than you are about the possible benefit to the person. If you know that what you're offering can help them, maybe even change their life in some positive way, don't you think it's selfish to keep it to yourself? Give the person a chance. Lay it out in a nonthreatening, noninvasive way. Come from the goodness in your heart.

It doesn't matter where I am, what I'm talking about, or who I'm talking to, I can always work the conversation around to what I want to talk about. You can, too. And no, I don't talk to everyone I meet. I don't chase them down and insist they listen to me. I *feel* my way along. If I don't want to talk to people about business when I go out, I don't. If I sense a person is someone I wouldn't want to deal with, I keep quiet. I can go for days or weeks doing other business things, then a spell hits me and I'm out spreading the word. Some days I even make a game of it and talk about my product or business to every person I come across.

6

Training

Oh My Gosh!
I Finally Signed Someone!
Now What?!

Now that you've finally found and signed someone (yikes!), what do you do?

You have absolutely nothing until this person is trained. The person should understand as much about the business as you do, they should know that you are training them to copy you, and you should help them to get at least two to three more good distributors signed under them, and two or three more under those people.

You think you've been working hard until now, don't you? Look at it this way: When you sign a new person, they have, in effect, hired you to work for *them* — to teach them all they need to know and help them get started. *Your* reward will come later.

Start with yourself. Are *you* trained?

MLM as an Art Form

Diving seriously into a multilevel business is like going to a specialized trade school. You may think you know about business and how to succeed, but believe me, you don't know multilevel. You must go back to school and learn the art of MLM. Yes, I think of MLM as an art form. In art:

- You have to build a sculpture that looks good and doesn't fall over.
- You need to place the pieces of a collage in just the right places for the right effects.
- You need to paint a picture that attracts people instead of making them nauseous.

Art is a skill, MLM is a skill. Just sloppily throw either one together, and generally you have a fine mess. Networking has certain rules and they need to be learned. Once learned and practiced, you can eventually become an old master.

A story to illustrate: My Aunt Janis began painting when I was a little kid. At five years old, I knew her work was atrocious. She specialized in oils that were always wet. Whenever the family would visit her, we'd have to remark politely about her paintings, remembering to keep our distance from all the monstrosities on the walls, those leaning against chairs, the ones on the back porch, and the unfinished piece on the bathroom ceiling. The worst one, I thought, was a nude man with a penis like a limp carrot.

I used to look at that picture and think, "Gosh Aunt Janis, you're really awful." I wondered why she persisted, year after year, when she had no talent, except one for making her relatives suffer. Well, she fooled me and taught me a lesson. Toward the end of her painting career, her works were hanging in galleries. Art shows with champagne were held in her honor! Once she hit the big time, she quit and took up writing. I didn't say a thing.

Right now you might be Aunt Janis. You may be perfectly awful in MLM and not even realize it, or, maybe you do. It doesn't matter, just keep learning and persisting until you can have your own champagne party.

There's a great idea that circulates in networking circles: You can't possibly fail in MLM unless your company lets you down, you're totally incompetent, or you quit too soon. Most people quit too soon — don't be one of those; learn the business, do the business, and eventually prosper.

Back to School

How do you fashion your own MLM trade school? Research and learn everything you can about MLM. Absorb every MLM book, tape, video, and flyer you can find. Oddly enough, they're not often in regular book stores, so you have to scout. You may have to buy directly from the authors. You might contact different people in various MLMs and ask what books they read, what tapes they listen to, and what videos they watch. Ask where they get them. When you do this, expect to get the person's business presentation. And what's wrong with that? You'll learn how other people work an MLM business. You'll observe and take notes, then practice different techniques and see what works for you.

One caution! Remember, if you have made a commitment to your present MLM, don't let anyone pull you away from it. *Above all*, don't try to divide your commitment between two MLMs. That undermines your purpose and weakens you. If you feel weak, stick with your own company. They should have educational tools, classes, and meetings. Use them and go to them!

There are different MLM newspapers that come and go. Find one and subscribe. *Money Maker's Monthly* is one.[1]

Join the MLMIA(Multi Level Marketing International Association).[2] It works to improve the public's idea of MLM. They can help you learn more about your new line of work.

Identify someone in your upline (no matter how far up!) who is succeeding. Ask them to be your mentor. Tell them how serious you are. If they have brains, they'll go all out to help you, no matter how far down from them you are. Remind them that those closer to them may fail and fall, as you, *The Worker,* advance ever closer to them in their downline (presuming that your company skips unproductive distributors in the monthly royalties tally). Call the "chosen ones" at least every few days and follow them around. Be a copycat.

My far up-upline told me an interesting tale about getting trained. For two and one-half years, Molly called a special friend of hers about our business. The woman kept sighing and saying, "No, no, no. I have a perfectly wonderful MLM already." Molly persisted, calling and mailing new information every month or so.

One day the lady called her, saying, "We have to talk. My wonderful MLM isn't so wonderful anymore." Molly was ecstatic. "So," continued the woman, "I'm 70 years old

---

[1] *Money Maker's Monthly*, P.O. Box 7116, Villa Park, IL 60181
   708-920-1118, FAX 708-920-8377
[2] MLMIA, 119 Stanford Ct., Irvine CA 92715

and haven't time to reinvent the wheel. Tell me exactly what you've done to be successful. Lay out every step and I'll follow, 1-2-3."

"Well," Molly said, "first, you need to become a Manager. That's about $4,000 worth of product."

"Done," said the woman.

"And next," Molly said, "you need to fly to our company business meeting and get pinned."

"Done," said the woman.

"Then, you need to fly to our next training and get trained."

"Done," said the woman.

Molly gasped when she told me this. "I couldn't believe it," she confided. "She was willing to copy, exactly, everything that has brought me success. She had no ego or other false trappings. She was completely teachable! I expect her to have the best group in my whole business."

Consider doing this yourself. Copy excellence. Later on, you can add your own embellishments. Too often, we try to improvise and embellish *first*, because we're sure we know so much. Then, as time passes and we don't succeed, we quit, convinced that MLM is a rake-off. We neglect to notice that our own egos blew us out.

Depression

If you're feeling discouraged and depressed, instead of saying, "Maybe I'm no good at MLM, maybe I'm a failure at this," say something different. Say, "Wait a minute. What do I need to do differently?" Or, "What do I need to change," or "What do I need to learn about MLM that I don't know yet?" Because that's what it might be, you know. You're not a failure or a dodo. You just don't understand MLM, yet. You're still in school, doing your homework and practicing.

For example, Alice called me this morning and said, "Tom and I have been doing this business for eight months." She practically cried. " I'm ready to quit. I just spent $1,300 mailing out flyers, and I didn't get one call!"

"First of all," I said carefully, "People will rarely call you from a mail-out. You have to do a follow-up call."

"Well," Alice said, "I can't do that. I bought the mailing list and it's only addresses"

"And," I continued, "I'd never buy a cold mailing list unless I felt sure there were some *live* people on it. It would also be great if the list included phone numbers. Those people would probably think my flyers were more junk mail from an unknown source, so I'd like to either call them first to let them know the information is coming, or call them later so they can pull it out of the trash.

Hopefully, Alice just learned two things about what often doesn't work in this business and added them to her mental file:

1. Call either before or after you send something.
2. Be cautious with purchased mailing lists.

Alice didn't know these things a week ago, but now she does. She's not a failure because she didn't know them.

We're two down and Alice is on to her next complaint about herself. "I'm a failure, Venus. So many of our downline aren't doing anything. Tom and I went out, found all these people, made them all managers, and we were so excited. Now look — we only have two left that do anything!"

"Here's something," I said, "that one of my downline taught me. After you sign someone, you have thirty days to train them before they get discouraged and drop out. By the end of a month, they've had a heap of rejections, their fantasies have dissolved, and their relatives have convinced them they're involved in yet another dumb thing. A huge percentage of people give up and drop out with even the best of care, but you can lessen that rate if you train them quickly and give them your support."

Alice moaned. "That's not our strong point," she said. "Tom and I can sign anyone, anywhere, but training is beyond me. It's so boring."

"Yes." I agreed. "You two are marvels at finding and signing people. I mean, look at this lady you signed yesterday. You'd just met her and twenty minutes later she bought $5,000 worth of product. But, what's she going to do with it, if you don't teach her? You're not a failure, Alice. You've just been refusing to master the next step in MLM, which is *Training*:

- Study those MLM books I gave you.
- Go to other people's trainings.
- Watch what I and the rest of your upline do.
- Hang out with us.
- Practice.

Renewed, Alice and I worked up a plan to train the people she and Tom were so adeptly raking in.

When building your business, do a lot of what you do best (like Alice was doing) while identifying, learning and practicing the other parts.

The only way you can be a failure is if you neglect to learn and master what you don't know.

What to Do with New Distributors Immediately

(95% of all new distributors will not do these things unless you hold their hands while they do them. But if they don't do these things, 95% will not succeed. That means *you* will not succeed!)

You did all these things when you signed up, so we're reviewing:

1. Get a commitment from them to work the business. Do this the second after you sign them. Have them write it down. For example: "I commit myself to one solid year of learning and working this business. *Nothing* will cause me to quit."

2. Make a wish list. The first thing you need to teach your distributors is to ask themselves: "What do I want my new business to do for me?" Then, have them write it all down. Tell them to take the list home and tack it on the wall. It will remind them why they're working so hard.

Those thought-out and written desires will keep them going. Otherwise, when they hit the rough spots on the MLM road, they'll be tempted to quit. Remember, you have a list like this, too — and you're training your distributors to copy you.

My distributors' wish lists show varying desires of what they want from MLM:
- *Joannie's* wish is to stop working at a department store.
- *Bill* wants to be totally debt free.
- *Joel* wants to be able to donate $5,000 a month to AIDS research.

- *Barbara* wants to help women own their own lives.
- *Joe* wants to travel, teach, and speak throughout the world.
- *Janet and Leo* want to take a month off every six months and take their kids on long vacations.
- *Rachel* wants a life of ease and travel. She wants her friends to have the money to join her, so she's getting them involved in her company, too.

3. Acquire product. Have your distributors purchase product right now. If they need training manuals or videos, have them purchase the materials from you now, and/or lend them videos to watch. Have them either buy the product from you, or order it as you listen.

If they go home without product, they go home without a business. Many groups say to a new person, "We'll expect you to sign up three people who'll agree to purchase a certain amount of product to get started. That will make you a Manager right away." Then they'll say, "And before we let those three people buy all that product, we'll help each of them find three key people on their prospect lists who will do the same thing."

Some groups expect this because that certain amount of product purchased will make your new person a Manager or Supervisor, or whatever your company calls someone who's making the best percentages. You may expect it; however, you may not get it. Your person may scream, "No, no, a thousand times, no! All I want is a box!" Do your best. If you have them order a lot of product, be prepared to help them move it. That same help also needs to be extended to all their distributors who are encouraged to purchase a lot of product initially.

4. Get a no-squirm-out promise from your new person to attend the next company meeting or training. Then, pick them up.

5. Make a prospect list. Look your new people in the eye and say, "Now, you'll need five to ten sharp people...like yourself." It's important to stress: *like yourself.*

Have your new distributors each write up a list of people (right then is a good idea). Then say, "O.K. Let me go over your list and help you identify the best three."

The best three will be people who have a strong desire or need to do the business, some money and time to do it, some business or MLM background, and persistence. However, it's possible they'll have none of that and will be the dark horse that wins the race. You never know, but you're at least trying to be sensible.

6. Set up a meeting. Immediately have your new distributors call (or write, then call and confirm) those three choice people, plus everyone else on their list. Tell your distributors to invite them over for a get-together, potluck, fun evening, or to meet a really fun person who has a unique idea (you!).

Be cautious with the word "meeting." People usually don't like meetings. They tend to think of homeowners association meetings, dry business lectures, or a conference with the boss when they hear the word "meeting." That's not how most people want to spend their evenings. However, don't be coy, either, and let them think that the bunch of you are going to drink beer all night long, get naked, and roll in bacon fat. They won't like it when you make them drink weak punch, keep their clothes on, and listen to some jerk talk about rouge and eyebrow colors. Let them know that you're using an intriguing product, it has a novel business concept, and there's *free food*.

Next, you need to show up to help give the meetings and sign new distributors under your new people. Your new distributors should watch how you do it, and learn by your example. Before you leave these meetings, make sure that all newly signed distributors have set dates for meetings at *their* homes.

You will attend those meetings set by the people you helped to sign that evening, as will your frontline people. This is how groups are built. Your downline is learning how to do presentations and handle sign-ups, by watching you.

Repeat this process of giving meetings until you feel assured that your frontliners can do this on their own. Then say, "Sally, you've now got five good frontline distributors from our meetings at your house and those five averaged six people each from their home meetings. Those thirty collectively picked up many more when they each had home meetings. It's time now for you to do this without me. You have five in your frontline, thirty in your second level, and even more in your third level. (This is the ideal situation, but it rarely happens.)"

Each frontline distributor has now provided you with many distributors, just through people he/she knows and the people they know. Some will be great, some O.K., and some will fall away.

Remember, help *all* of your first-level people hold meetings, and teach them to do the same with their new people. Make sure everyone teaches everyone else down the line. This should keep you busy for a good long while!

Your upline *should* be teaching you how to do this, as well as helping and training your frontline people too. But wait! They aren't? Do you have a lousy, distant, or uneducated upline? So what! Begin with yourself. Do it on your own. Learn as you go. Be honest. Tell the group you're nervous, but this is such a great opportunity, you're willing to jump your fear.

7. Make appointments. Instead of meetings, a different approach is to help your new distributors set up personal appointments with prospects. Look through the prospect lists and help your distributors single out a few to call or contact. Be prepared to go with your distributors to the appointments. It can be as simple as Sally (your distributor) calling and saying to her friend, "Marcy, I'm thinking about committing my life to a new business and I value and need your opinion. Let's have lunch (or coffee) and we can talk. I'll have a friend with me. What day this week are you free?" Or you can go to her house.

After you sign Marcy into the business , tell her to set up appointments with her friends. You and Sally and Marcy will then meet with them, so the two ladies can see how you do a presentation. Tell Sally and Marcy you'll do this with them two days a week for three to four weeks until they get the hang of it. Work with the rest of Sally's distributors and help them the same way. Before you know it, you will have more distributors than you dreamed, and you will also begin to have a solid, producing group.

Train Sally this way and assure her that you will meet with her or talk to her once a week, just to keep on track. Now, *you* go find and sign two or three other frontline distributors and repeat the entire process.

P.S. Be creative. If you can think of a better way to find and train distributors, do it. As you know, I generally find and train people wherever they fall. For example: When I meet someone, I casually mention my business or products — and then just happen to have a sign-up kit and products in the car. They're in business.

I'll often say to my downline "If you've got someone you want me to talk to, call them first and tell them about me and what I've got. Then I'll call them." I often help my distributors by speaking to their prospect over the phone — answering questions and so forth.

Another Way to Say the Same Thing: Draw Up a Blueprint

I learned the following by a pool in Acapulco. (I was on an all-expenses-paid business trip!) I came home with invaluable information (and the Mexican Quick-step, which is a debilitating form of diarrhea), but I feel the trip was well worth it, because I also learned about *blueprints*. John (a sweetheart of a guy in MLM) graciously shared his knowledge as he explained the following to me. I have loosely strung it together for you. Fit it in when you're training your new people.

Everyone needs a *blueprint* to build an MLM business, just as you would for a house, or like you would need a pattern for a dress. Once you set up a blueprint, or pattern, your people can follow it.

1. Ask your new prospect or distributor, "How much money do you need or want to make per month from this opportunity?" If the person doesn't know, ask if they'd take a job without knowing the salary.

Some people will say, "Gee, $500 a month would be great." Others will quote $1,000, $6,000, or $25,000. Take an extra look at the big thinkers. They're half-way there.

2. Whatever amount the person says, map out how they can make that kind of money in your company. For example:

- How many pots will their group have to move every month to make your friend that $500 or $2,000?
- How many tubes of face cream?
- How many life insurance policies need to be sold by how many of their downline each month to make them $1,000 a month?

Pencil the details out for each person. Help them determine exactly how much of what must be moved every month to bring in the desired income.

3. The next step with this blueprint is: *How do they get these items moving?* The answer:

a. Start by finding three to five good, strong frontline people and help them find people.

b. Next, identify the strongest people downline in each leg of your three to five frontline distributors. Look as far down as each leg goes to find them. Write down their names and phone numbers.

c. Contact your three to five frontline distributors and ask them to contact these people you've identified. Call them yourself, as well, and tell them: "You're one of the key people in my organization. I'm going to really work with you to help you build your business. Now I want you to identify your three strongest people, so I can work with them, too.

What Happens When You Don't Train?

Some of us are really good at getting distributors. We sign 'em up, tell them to study the materials and go to meetings, then we dash off to find new prospects. While we're doing that, the distributors crash, tumble, whither on the stick, and disappear. A once promising, or even flourishing group disintegrates, leaving us stunned and perplexed. Often we sign and run because we think our distributors are just like us: self-motivated, able hardworkers who will figure it out and do it on their own. Some of us think we know how to train and won't listen to our upline or our compny's suggestions. Whatever the reasons, it's death to your business not to train.

Miscellaneous Notes

Here are a few more things you can do to help and train your people:

1. Get all appropriate information to your people immediately and teach them to do the same. How can your group survive if they don't know anything, or know what's going on within the company? My checks doubled when I started mailing newsletters. Put aside your ego and laziness. Add to the information if you want, but pass along what you receive from your upline.

2. Call your people constantly. "What's your program for the day? How much product do you plan to move this month? What are your goals in this business?" Tell them the latest inspiring news and what you are doing to promote your business. Remember one cardinal rule: Always *encourage* your downline. If you feel miserable, call your upline.

3. Train your people to call you daily to check in. You'll soon find who's serious and who you should work with. As Smiley, a man in my downline told me, "When I was in another MLM, we called each other everyday." He thought for a moment, then, "At least, those of us who succeeded did."

4. Give your distributors all the information they need to get started. Tell your people what they need to know. Give them books, audios, or use flyers (such as the one below) to let them know exactly what they need to do to create a viable MLM business.

There's a Million Things Your Babies Need to Know

1. Teach your people how to sign three to five people, and teach their downline to copy them.
2. Teach your people to write and run ads.
3. Help your people set up their work space.
4. Teach your people the intricacies of the marketing plan.
5. Explain how to get people to meetings.
6. Explain how to order from the company.
7. Teach your people how to lean on their upline.
8. Tell your people where to get MLM training materials. Better yet, supply them.
9. Give your people my book, *MLM Magic*, and any other relevant training material.

You have to be there for your people as they learn to walk and as they ask questions. In the beginning, in a sense, you even have to carry them to meetings!

An easy way to train them is to give them this book and insist they get copies of it to their new people too. (Yes, I know my suggestion is blatant advertising, but when you're writing your own book, you can put anything you want in it.) Actually, I was driven to write this book because so many people have asked me, "How did you build your business. Can you tell me in five minutes?" Now I can say "Sure. Read the book." (There are good discounts offered for quantity orders. Your upline and your distributors may want to order this book together with you, in order to get the best discount. You can do this with other MLM books, also).

Once again, if you have never been trained, get trained. Hopefully, you know how to accomplish that now, because your people are relying on you.

Turn to your upline. Find and call your five immediate upline managers. Tell them your goals. Ask them to support you. If some are worthless, keep going until you find the good ones. Also, give your downline the names and numbers of their responsible upline, and tell your people to call them. Use your upline, copy their successful patterns, and let them be mentors to you.

Be sure each of your distributors has a copy of the checklist for new distributors on the following page.

Checklist for
New Distributors

☐ Commit to the business.
☐ List what you want the business to do for you.
☐ Order product.
☐ Make a prospect list.
☐ Attend company-sponsored meetings, and the training meetings given by upline.
☐ Get an answering machine.
☐ Study MLM training materials in your company's distributor kit, plus any audios, videos, or books about MLM that you can find.
☐ Learn how to call people.
☐ Learn how to do a presentation.
☐ Give a home meeting. Learn how to sign up people.
☐ Consider getting an 800 number, if you have out of the area distributors
☐ Carry product in your car.

Building
Your Business

Baby Your Babies

Training and building your group often seems to be the same thing, so there will be some repetition in this section. It's important to absorb it well, though; your MLM business revolves around people. Most people are infants in MLM. In other words, they have had little or no previous experience with it.

As soon as you sign new people, treat them as if they were just born, like babies who need to learn everything...because they do. Call them constantly. One man in my group who is very successful calls his people every day. Do this forever, or at least until you get the feeling they never want to hear from you again. If I start sensing that, I ask them, "Do you want me to keep helping you? Have you lost interest? I'm so busy, I need to know if I should keep working with you."

Always look way downline for serious people. There may be a gem six or twelve levels removed. When you take the time to find and work with these people, most of the time there's a big payoff. Either they inspire all the people under you in their upline, or else everyone above them drops out and you suddenly have "Miss Major Mascara Mover" right under *your* nose.

Right now, I have in my group a lady named Kathy who used to be seven levels down from me. She's now my first level, and what a winner! She's a widow with two years' worth of money left. She tells me, "Venus, I *have* to make this work." I love to hear that. She has a driving reason to succeed. She doesn't want to eat cat food in her eminent old age. After a number of false starts and starting all over again, she's now well on her way. Thank goodness she got my newsletters and we worked together when she was seven levels down from me!

Monitor and work with your serious people at least three levels deep (and more is better). Keep looking downline as I've said, and make a note of anyone who should be encouraged. If you have managers who have become stone cold or are flopping their last, definitely see who should be saved below them. Become those people's foster parent. It pays to deeply cultivate the ground beneath your feet.

You've now looked through your growing downline and noted who's strong, who isn't, and who needs your help. There's a caution here: When you have a good strong leg or person, there's a temptation to let them do their own thing, while you slap and grease the weaker ones along. That's a mistake. Encourage your good people *first*. Call them first. Everybody gets discouraged and everybody has slow times. Wouldn't it be awful to lose your best line because of your neglect?

In my office I have several pages of lined paper encased

in plastic sheets. The name of the strong lead dog, and the names of two or three key people in each leg are written out.

- Each name has a phone number and address.
- Each of these people is on my direct mailing list for my newsletters.
- Each person talks to me at least twice a week (often because they call me), although I talk to some every day. They are the first to hear the latest news and the most exciting ideas. We work closely together in every possible way. They keep me enthused and filled with new and workable ideas, and hopefully I do the same for them.

Take care of everyone else with newsletters, calls, postcards and voice box messages, to be explained later, but give most of your time to those who deserve it. This idea of working with the three key people in each leg is easy. If you have ten legs, you're only working closely with thirty people.

Miscellaneous Business-building Notes

Here's a loose collection of ideas that come from different brilliant minds and sources, none of which I can remember and give accurate credit to. Some come from my own brilliant mind, of course:

- If you have to convince someone to get in the business, you'll have to convince them to stay in the business.
- Coming and going is easy (in and out of an MLM company). It's the staying that's hard.
- Regarding developing a multilevel: Design a life. Don't just earn a living.
- Only one-half of one percent of all people make more than $50,000 a year. You can make that in one month

in the right MLM.
- Only work with those who deserve your help.
- Just jump in and DO IT.
- Look for people with accents. They work harder.

A Few More Ideas

Send postcards or notes to those in your downline who are doing well. For example, "I've noticed how great you're doing. I'll be keeping an eye on your progress. You're terrific, Lisa!"

When you're vacationing on company money, send a postcard. Awhile back I sent one of my ladies a card from Hawaii. It featured a handsome, tan, and almost nude Hawaiian man. "Tina," I wrote, "guess what I'm doing over here? You'll have to be with me next year!"

Tina told me she kept that card on her refrigerator for nine months as she slobbered and drooled over the future trip. "That's what pushed me to do the volume to get here," she said, as we lolled on the beach in Hawaii a year later.

Call those who are doing well. "Hi Jack, I'm your way upline, Venus. We haven't met, but I noticed on my company printout that you sold fifty cases of product last month. I'm sure glad you're in my group. Anything I can do for you?" If there isn't, at least blow tinsel in his ears.

WIIFM: What's In It For Me? That's what everyone wants to know about the multilevel you're hoping they'll join. Tell them.

Remember the "Tortoise and the Hare" story? Think of it while you're building your business. The payoff is where you are at the end of the race...not how long it takes to get there. What do you care if it takes you longer to get the hang of MLM and you retire in five or six years, instead of two? Where would you be in six years if you didn't have your MLM business?

- Say "Next" as you play the numbers game, looking for the right people.
- Send copies of both your and your upline's checks to your downline every month.
- Your car is a rolling university. Listen to training tapes, company tapes, positive tapes. Teach yourself your new line of work while you're driving to and from the future old one.
- Buy sticky labels with your name and phone number printed on them, or make your own by stamping your name and phone number in ink onto blank stickers. Then, stick them on all your products. People often can't remember where they got things.
- Carry some product and distributor kits in your car. You never know where you'll find business.
- Match negative thoughts with their opposite.
- Like I've said before, look for people who were child entrepreneurs. Ask, "Did you have a lemonade stand as a kid? Sell candy bars, etc.?" If they were entrepreneurial that far back, then it's still in them. Go after it.
- You must constantly look for new people in this business to replace those who fade away. If you keep working with those who stay but aren't growing, they can become your stumbling blocks.
- Always have more prospects than you have time to call.
- Tell your downline: "There's only one way I'll have time to help you with this business. You have to show me that you want to make this work." Then watch their actions.
- Plan out your MLM life at least every two weeks. Maybe what you planned previously didn't work; make changes.

Your first four to eight months in a multilevel are, generally, the hardest. (It's often longer if you're new to MLM). When things get rough, start to pretend; go sit in a new Mercedes, try on that dress made of diamonds. Take a day off and pretend that every day is like this.

One last note: People who succeed are "Movers and Shakers." They get themselves trained, they don't wait for it to be done for them.

Ideas to Make You Look Good

Collect business cards from people in all lines of work who belong to your MLM. They don't need to be in your group. When you're hoping to sign a policeman, a doctor, or an artist, whip out your book of cards and point to all the appropriate ones. People like to feel they're in good company.

Take a camera to every company meeting or function. Get a shot of yourself with six doctors, another with you looped arm in arm with the *Single Mom who Made Good*, and a batch with you and the old mother who developed the company's star product, "Greasy Granny's Hair Ball Remover."

Spread these pictures out in front of new prospects. There you are, arm in arm with the founding father, and his two clever single daughters who are worth millions. And there you lie, drunk as a pipe, on the beaches of Bimini with the similarly indisposed "Company All-Stars." And next, you are immortalized, hot but happy, touring the company plant in Leafwort, Texas, with two boxes of flattened product squeezed under your armpits.

Who wouldn't be impressed?

More on Building

Chris is twenty-three and bright. He's used to wearing sober business suits and polished shoes. In his former line of work he wore a necktie so tight it made his head look like a poppy pod. Now he's doing MLM full time. He's determined to make his fortune with us and to do all the work it takes.

"At first," he said, "every morning I'd put on my coat, sharp pants, and tie. I'd slick back my hair and wipe off my black leather briefcase, snap my heels together and shoot out my front door. I was a businessman and I went out to prospect the owners of retail businesses. Unfortunately, they'd see me coming and dart behind their desks, or hide in the back room. I got depressed. What was I doing wrong? I looked great. I smelled good. I had a professional approach. Why was everyone so cool to me?

"Then I remembered you, Venus. You break most of the rules. You dress casually. Your hair flies out to the sides of your head and you grin a lot. I've never seen you carry a briefcase. I remember once overhearing your upline beg you to wear a dress to a meeting. You once told me that people aren't afraid of you, that they relate to you as one of them. Most of the time, they never guess that you're going to punch a hole through their heads and change their thinking and their lives. So I said 'O.K.'

"The next day I put on my nice jeans, a casual shirt, and cowboy boots. I left my briefcase at home. I was nervous with my new approach, but guess what? No one was nervous with me. The business managers, sales people, and owners sidled right up to me. I kept my hands casually in my pockets and just chatted about wanting to meet everyone in my neighborhood. Gradually, I'd get into my business, and then we'd talk about their business. I had a ball. Now I go out every day to see my neighborhood friends. Many of them have signed up with me."

Free Counseling is
Part of the Business

Last night, three of my downline called and begged me to contact one of the distributors in their group. Martha Mary had locked herself in her bedroom with a major depression and boils all over her face.

"She says she's quitting the business," Linda told me. "Please, Venus, you've got to stop her! She's worked so hard at this, don't let her quit now."

Five minutes later Rodney called, "Please, Venus, Martha Mary is really upset this time. A big MLMer promised he'd sign with her, but he signed with someone else. Please call her right away!"

Ten minutes later, Alice was on the line, "Venus, Martha Mary's the worst I've seen her. You know how great she is in this business, but she's taken to her room with the worst case of acne and hormones I've ever seen. She says she's never coming out. Just between us Venus, I know what's wrong with her. She's a thirty-four-year-old virgin, and you have to talk to her about that."

"And what am I supposed to say?" I asked.

"Well, you know Venus, she thinks God's against sex since she's not married, and not ever having sex is making her crazy. It's ruining her business and we all want you to talk to her about this."

In MLM, I counsel numbers of people every day, and you will too. It's part of building the business, so you might as well get good at it.

Today I talked to Martha Mary about her hormones. After that, Denise called to tell me about her daughter, who apparently had called the TV cable company while Denise was out and had them install not only cable, but all the pay channels as well, then ran off with Denise's car. Denise was tight with anger when I spoke with her. I said, "Oh you'll get your chance at her. You know she's coming back to watch that cable."

I yelled at Tom and told him he'd better start paying back what he owes his downline, because they're all calling me.

I heard about Diane's near fatal car accident last night.

I told Mark to come down and spend the day with me so I could teach him everything about MLM that his sponsor refused to.

Robin complained of dizzy spells for three weeks and asked for advice. We decided she'd been taking too many Epsom salt baths.

Phil wanted to know if he should be getting so much gas.

Nancy was having trouble with her copy machine and her boyfriend. What did I suggest?

With a day like this, why should I balk at counseling an old virgin? You'll need to be ready to do the same.

My Typical Day

My downline often asks me, "What's a typical day for you, Venus?" I guess they think that if they do just what I do, they'll be successful. Maybe they're right! Here's a regular day of mine when I first started my current MLM several years ago:

7:00 a.m.
- I'm showered, dressed, I've had my tea and quiet thinking or happy reading time, and am now in my kitchen office.
- If I can think of anyone to call this early, I will.
- Otherwise, I'm planning out the day and writing it down.
- Maybe I'm writing up a newsletter, too, or a new informative flyer.

8:00 a.m.

- As the day progresses, I try to fit in breakfast.
- Sometimes I rearrange and clean up my work area.
- Other times, I attempt to remember everyone I ever knew so I can write, or call them about my new business.

9:00 a.m. to noon

- I call my downline and set up times to get together, or discuss their key people and how we can help them.
- Sometimes I write up ads, listen to a training tape, watch a company video for inspiration, or read an MLM or sales book.
- If I have ad calls coming in at a certain time, I stay home and wait for them, or, I redo the recorded message I have waiting for callers.
- Sometimes I sit outside and think about what working in this MLM will do for me.

12:00 noon to 1:30 p.m.

- Sometimes I take a prospect to lunch. When I'm buying, they can't complain about what I talk about...and I talk business.
- I might plan a home meeting with some of my downline for their new prospects and mine.

1:30 p.m. to 7:00 p.m.

- Some days, I go people hunting. That might mean grocery or clothes shopping, or just out sitting and watching.
- I may send postcards to my downline to keep them inspired, or call a retail person to see how well they liked the product.
- At least every other day I'll call my upline's voice-mail box to hear about new developments in the company, or information on local meetings.

- Maybe I call or go see someone in my upline (or someone else's). I want to be around and absorb success.

7:00 p.m.

- Tonight might be a Mexican do at Therese's house with our products mixed in with the hot sauce.
- Of course, I go to every meeting and class that anyone in my company lets me come to. I'll drive miles for a drop of knowledge. I'll even go to other company's meetings to see how they operate! (I never get caught in another MLM, though. I'm loyal to mine.)
- Maybe I'm in bed by eleven, but it's with a book in hand. Usually it's something that will help me with my business, or help me grow as a person. Generally, I'm so absorbed in my work and plans that I dream about the business all night!

(And by the way, all the above was worked around a "real job" that I worked from my home!)

That was my typical twenty-four hours. Are you willing to do that for two to three years, *or more*, to buy your freedom for life?

The Basics

Meetings

It's Monday at 5:00 p.m. After a full day, I'm bleaching some clothes in the bathroom sink, and another load is in the washer. Dinner is partly fixed and Summer has a 5:30 dental appointment. The dentist insists we have to slice off half her head, remove five teeth, and put her in a head brace. I'm going on this appointment to demure. At 7:30 I have to be at yet another MLM meeting. I'd rather be at home.

People complain a lot about going to meetings: "Sorry, I've got to be at a psychic faire," they moan. Or, "Gee, I don't know about that night. My dog has fleas." Or, more common, "Yep! I'll see you there!" — and they never show.

Someone was complaining to me once that their business was going nowhere. "I don't see you at the meetings," I said mildly.

"Come on, Venus," my downline answered, "do *you* like going to those meetings?"

"Of course not!" I told her. "But I go. And after I'm

there, I actually enjoy myself. Not only that, if I don't give and go to meetings, my alternative (and yours) is a nine-to-five job (forever, maybe — unless I'm fired), a watch at retirement (maybe), and a $700-dollar-a-month pension (maybe)."

You and your people should hit every meeting that's held, anywhere, until you know everything about your company and your product. Then, attend at least one meeting a week to keep yourselves revved up. Again, professional MLMers say, "Never go to a meeting without one new person." Venus says, "Go by yourself if you're all you've got." I've attended scores of meetings by myself. I do it to stay excited and to stay in touch.

How Do I Do a Meeting?

Home meetings are often the best. For one thing, if nobody shows up, you haven't gone anywhere...and you haven't paid $200 for a hotel meeting room, either. Don't rent a room until you have a solid group you can count on, with a few downline who will share the cost.

Some people hold open house several times a week. Maybe it's every Tuesday and Thursday in the evenings, and Saturday morning. Distributors and prospects can come by and get training, product, or just attention. Maybe every Monday night you have a regular meeting, no matter what. If people show, you do a meeting. If not, you spend the evening wondering why, and making plans to get people to the next one.

Personally, I like having tea parties — like the one I mentioned in Chapter Four. I'll call four to five of my downline, new distributors or old ones who need some help or encouragement with the business, and say, "I'm having a tea party Thursday at 2:00 p.m. Can you come? Can you bring a prospect or two?" People like to come to these. We sit in the sunshine in my living room. I serve tea in brightly painted cups, we eat crumbly, obnoxiously healthy cookies, and my overbearing yellow cat makes rude remarks. A lot of training and work gets done. We discuss any aspect of the business that's brought up. We make plans and get excited.

Some of you executive-types may be laughing about these tea parties...but you'd choke instead if you could see my monthly checks. So, get out your lace tablecloths and tea bags, fellows. Tea is at two.

The Agenda

The following meeting outline depends on your company and product, of course, but loosely, a meeting might run like this:

You've signed up a brand new distributor, Mary Lou. The day she signed you had her draw up a list of prospects. Then you helped her call and invite them to a meeting at her home. She might have promised her friends a barbecue, a tea party with crumpets, or hinted that you would set yourself on fire with a stick. Maybe she used guilt — whatever it took to get them there. You've also asked your new prospects to attend. Why not? You might as well fling the same stone at a bunch of birds, yours included. It saves having a separate meeting for your new prospects.

- Start on time. Why let the latecomers dictate to you and those who are prompt?
- Ask for names. It's nice to have everyone give their names and say something about themselves, or why they think they're here. ("My wife forced me," or "I don't want to be here, and I'm leaving as soon as possible," or "I owe my buddy, here, a favor," or "You

made me feel guilty," and so on.)

- Tell your company and product story.
- If you have a company video, show it.
- Give samples of your products to those who haven't tried them, or show people how they work, or whatever. If any of your upline or downline is there (be sure to invite them!), ask them to share their experiences with the product, the company, and their lives.
- Offer an opportunity: Mention that you are now going to show the new people an opportunity, and that afterwards you will ask if in fact they see one. "If you don't," you say, "that's fine and dandy. We won't press you about it, but we thank you for coming to check it out. You can hit the cookie and punch table if you want to before you leave." Then, proceed to outline your opportunity and the marketing plan. Make it simple and short. If you get too many sticks and balls rolling across the chalkboard, you'll lose people.
- Follow up on your promise. Ask if anyone sees an opportunity here. Thank those that don't, and let them escape.

Sign 'em Up

Work individually with those people who do see a business opportunity and want to sign up. Begin by whipping out your distributor sign-up kit, or whatever your company uses. I like to dramatically slice it open, dump out its innards, and just quickly run through the contents.

"Let me just show you what's here," I state, as I snatch out the distributor application and slide it under their nose. "Here's where you put your name and address," I say, as I hand them a pen. "What do you want to do?" I don't like to fiddle for hours with a person. Generally, they know what they want or they don't. Sometimes, however, they want to run home and ask Uncle Harry or their wife for advice.

If they do, their relatives will usually batter them into submission with, "Don't tell me you've fallen for another flimflam scam! Remember the last stupid deal you got into? I've heard about this one! If you do it, I'll divorce you (disown you, muddy your name within the family, cause you great embarrassment, harass you about your gullibility, and so on)."

So, it's better to sign them at the moment if you can. Their relatives will still pounce on and throttle them, but the person has *you* now, as a friend and ally to help hold the hordes at bay.

I have often found, however, that if a person doesn't have the inner qualities to know what's good for them and what *they* want to do, against all family objections, then they probably aren't worth bringing into your group, anyway.

Remember, a meeting with new people should not be a hustle-bustle, hurdy-gurdy, sign 'em up quick schitck. Present the products and the opportunity with dignity. If it's right for the people, they'll buy or sign up. If it's not, they'll keep looking, and so should you.

One-on-one Meetings

Let's say Mary Lou has just unfurled her list of prospects before you. You've just signed her up, and she's anxious to make a million by tomorrow.

1. First of all, carefully go through the list with her. Ask her who she thinks:

    a. Has the most desire to make some money?

    b. Would manufacture an extra six to ten hours a week to work the business?

    c. Needs the product the most?

2. Question her closely about these people. You may know better than she who the most likely prospects are.

3. Then, as you sit there, have her call several of these most likely people and set appointments to see them.

You want to start with the most likely people first, because we want to minimize new distributor discouragement. Prospects who say no somehow have an adverse affect on a new distributor! So, how does Mary Lou get an appointment?

Each person, with practice, will find the right technique for him or her. Until that happens, Mary can use other people's proven techniques, such as the following:

- "Hi, Tom? This is Mary Lou. I've always valued your opinion and would like to have it now. I'm considering a new line of work and would like your input. You might be interested in it also. Would you meet me for coffee? What's the closest coffee shop to your work? And what days are you not free this week?" (That way you don't dance around in circles looking for an open day!) "I'll have a friend with me." (That's you, her sponsor.)

- "Toni, I've just learned about a great way to make some extra money. Let's have lunch tomorrow, O.K? I'll buy. And, I'm bringing a friend with me."

- "Harry, where do you eat lunch? I've got something I want to run by you, but not on the phone."

Set the meeting up in the evening, or during the weekend, if that works for you. However, I don't like to do either. I like to relax at night and on the week-ends, and since I think most people do, I stick with lunch or tea.

Suppose your friend says, "Hey, what is this? Some multilevel scam?" You could say, "It might be. That's why

I want your opinion." Most people's ego will drag them clear out to Mozambique, so it should be easy to get them to a coffee shop right next to their work.

4. After you've set the appointment, send a postcard, "It was great talking to you. See you Tuesday at Camel Jake's.

5. If someone calls to cancel, reschedule the appointment right then. If a friend or prospect doesn't show, be glad. They weren't right for a business where it takes certain qualities to be successful.

6. What do you do with new prospects once you get them there? If you're Mary Lou, you sit and listen to your sponsor. If your sponsor isn't there, do what they would do: Be casual and frank while discussing your product and/or company. It's also good to bring samples with you, if that's possible.

7. The first thing you *don't* do is batter new prospects with your fabulous MLM. Ask questions about them instead:
- What kind of work do you do?
- What do you like about it?
- What don't you like about it?
- You seem like you'd be really good with people. (Always give a compliment.) Were you born this way, or did you learn techniques?
- What do you know about network marketing? You're probably very good at what you do...but I bet you'd be open to a better offer?

There's a man in my current MLM who does extremely well. His favorite sentence is, "Ask so many questions that prospects load your gun for you. Then you know exactly what to say to shoot and bag them."

When you have the facts, present your opportunity. Harry has just told you that he's fifty-eight and suddenly realizes he has almost nothing for retirement. You can mention that by working MLM part-time, he could eventually easily make an extra $1,000 a month. If he saved that $1,000 every month, in a year he'd have $12,000. With $12,000 down, he might be able to buy a little rental house. For the next five years he could collect rent to make the payments. After five years the house may have tripled in value, and he can rent it for more or sell it. Either way, he's got a lot more money. Plus, he's been making that extra $1,000 a month for those five years — and probably a lot more because his MLM business has grown during that time.

Or maybe you're sitting and chatting with Lenore. You find out that she wants to leave her rotten husband. She has told you that she married the wrong man, but now she's stuck because she doesn't make enough to survive without him. "Well Lenore, many women have started this business part-time. After a short while they felt secure enough and made enough money to leave the old buzzards. How soon can you pull a meeting together?"

"Help! My Sponsor's Not Here to Help Me Do These Meetings!"

Then do them on your own. You can do it. Your future is at stake. You *have* to do it!

Drop-ins vs. Appointments

You don't have to make yourself nervous by setting up an appointment. Remember, you can mention your product or business anytime, anywhere, with anyone. If you're dropping by Aunt Grace's house with the kids just to say hello and visit, happen to have some company literature and product samples with you in the car, and be sure to bring your new business into the conversation. Ask Aunt Grace and all the kids to let you slap that hot coral pancake make-up on them, or whip up an omelet in your sterling silver pot set, then encourage them to eat it. Let them know that they too can have the fun that you're having, and make tons of money, just by signing up with you.

You can also just happen to run into good ol' Mike as he's leaving for his coffee break or for lunch — or is looking as if he'd like to. "Mike, old buddy! Haven't seen you since high school! What a lucky break for you; I have something to tell you about! Can you get away for coffee, now?"

A lady I know is really good at the drop-in meeting. She just stops to chat and says midway through the conversation, "Oh! Could you help me out? My VCR is broken and I have this real short video I need to watch. Could I watch it here?" Of course her friend says yes, and of course, the video is all about this really exciting multilevel she's just joined.

How to Get People to Meetings

You can have set meetings on a regular basis (every Monday night for example), or have a special one for a new distributor who's just getting started. Have your new person invite everyone he/she's ever known to this meeting. Invite sixty and expect three. Advise him/her to send a company brochure with an invitation and a note that says, "I'll call you in three days, and if you're a *really* good friend, you'll be here, even though you don't want to be!" Then, call them.

I still use guilt to get people to a meeting. "Can I count on you to be there?" I plead. "Do I have your promise? Your commitment? You'll support me in this?" Use words like that, because when it comes to the night of the meeting, that armchair of theirs is just so comfortable, but if they know you're counting on them....

Another approach is: "Look, I'm thinking about committing myself to a new line of work. Would you come to a meeting and tell me what you think? I value your opinion." Or try, "I just got involved in this new business and I need to practice the marketing plan. Would you come to a meeting and tell me what you think?" Just be honest.

If they say, "Is this another stupid MLM meeting!?"

Say, "Yes, maybe, that's why I want you there to help me decide whether it's stupid or not." Logically, you'll have to think of a new method when you're making $200,000 a year.

Food, as I've mentioned before, is a good draw. If you don't mind having juice stains on your couch pillows and cookie chunks rolled across your white carpets, you'll pull more people with the promise of food. One lady serves chicken dinners. "It's easy to fix," she says, "and I get a big crowd." There's still some question as to what point in the gathering to feed people, however. If the meeting comes first, then they can't take their eyes off the food table. If the meeting comes after the food, three-quarters of the group will flee for the door before the meeting starts. "Just remembered I left my iron plugged in," or, "Gee, I'd love to stay, but I think that hot sauce gave me diarrhea," or, "Gosh, I've got an awful headache, got to run home to bed; great dinner, though." The only ones who stay are generally your mother, the person who's committed to wash the dishes, and the people who live there.

Speaker Phone Meetings

Sometimes one of my downline in Meltfoot, Montana, or Oakburst, Wisconsin, will call and ask me to fly out and do a meeting. "How many people can you pull together?" I suspiciously ask.

"Oh, maybe six," they say with great enthusiasm. "Unless Wilbur and Irene can't come."

From experience, I know that sometimes they'll be lucky to get just one to show (which is no reflection on Meltfoot or Oakburst; it's just how meetings can be, and that's O.K., especially if the one person who shows is a good one).

"I'll tell you what I can do," I tell my distributor. "Go to a place that sells phones and pick up a speaker phone. They cost about $40.00 and easily attach to your telephone. Let me know when your meeting is, and that night when you have all your people gathered, dial my number and flip on your new gadget. We can have a two-way conversation, a regular meeting, with the whole room. We'll all be able to hear each other."

I find this works very well. When the group is actually large enough to be worth spending your time and money on, *then* take your body out there.

Conference Calls

Call your operator about this. Your phone company can hook you and your downline together on one call. For example, you could have forty people on a call while you give them the latest training or company information. Make it a point to have these calls on a certain fixed date every couple of weeks, or every month. If you know you're going to be at an exciting company function in an exotic locale, let your downline know. At the agreed upon date and time, call them with all the news. You'll have them feeling desperate to build their (your) business so they can be there with you next time.

Consider having conference calls with only three to four people as well. Maybe you're hoping to sign up a chiropractor. Have two other chiropractors on the call that are in your MLM business. This will make your new person feel more confident about your company. The other two people will be glad to help you because they know you'll help them sometime. Again, call your phone company about this type of service.

Great Big Meetings

Meetings can take over your life and strangle your business. The ones I'm referring to are the ones that you, your downline, upline, sidelines, and sometimes even your company are involved in. These are the associations that generally put on weekly meetings, often in hotels.

They're the ones with presidents, secretaries, treasurers, heads of committees, and boxes of paperwork. They're usually wonderful for distributors and prospects, but these meetings can squeeze the business blood out of you and all those intimately concerned. The time you should be devoting to building your MLM becomes time devoted to setting up and arranging chairs, selling tickets to events, coordinating with hotel schedules, fighting with each other, finding speakers, and setting up and running trainings.

I love these groups, though. I love to send and take my people to their functions, but I choke when one of my downline says they're going to start, or work with one.

These groups are great assets to your business. I wouldn't want to be without them. Support and help them as best you can without sacrificing your future freedom to them.

800 Numbers

Having an 800 toll-free telephone number can be a great idea if you advertise. You can place ads all over the country and people can call this toll-free number to get more information on the product or business opportunity.

When someone calls, you can either answer the phone directly (but don't do this unless you like talking nonstop, mainly to people who will have no interest in your MLM), or the call can be fed into your answering machine or a voice-box number.

If you've chosen either of the latter two options, be sure to have a recorded message that piques curiosity and sifts out people who would waste your time. Ask the caller to leave their name, number, and the best time to reach them if they are still interested and want to know more. This really helps to weed out the serious from the nonserious.

To get an 800 number, call your operator or find one of the many alternative companies that offer 800 numbers. I once used an independent phone company. It was cheaper, but I got a lot of calls I couldn't account for. It might be better to go with a well-established company, although there is a drawback: it can be expensive.

My mother has an 800 number. She often gets wrong numbers which go on her bill. One time someone called, or rather *thought* they called, United Press — at four in the morning to report a homicide in Colombia. Also, people don't always check their numbers: One morning she got *three* calls for Hertz Rent-a-Car from the same person. I guess this person thought *she* was wrong.

Unless you do a lot of business all over the country, or plan on doing a lot of out-of-state advertising, you probably won't need an 800 number.

Voice Boxes or Voice Mail Systems

A voice box is a recorded communication system that's available from independent companies, and perhaps even regular phone companies by now. The company provides a phone line and number. When your calls come in, the voice box with your message on it springs into action, and callers get your prerecorded message, and can often leave a message in return if they want. A voice box acts like an extended answering machine, except that the phone isn't ringing at your house all day long, and you often have four or five minutes, or longer, to record an outgoing message.

Be sure to check out as many companies as you can before you sign up. Talk to customers of the companies to find out if they're satisfied. I had some problems with my former voice box company. The rate suddenly went up without warning, and the time limit for recording my message was cut. No one bothered to notify me of these changes! Otherwise, the voice box is a great idea.

Another plan is to run a second phone line into your house and connect an answering machine to it to take messages from your ads, or for your downline to call to get the latest news.

Every Monday I change the information on my current voice box. It's kept up to date with the latest meetings, trainings, and company gossip. Each week I attempt to fit in some training or words of encouragement. A voice box is a good way to keep in touch with your downline without having to call each of them down to the 26th generation. Actually, many other groups and lines call into my voice box. Sometimes I feel like a radio star. Consider getting a voice box. It will expand your business and feed your ego needs.

The Telephone

The phone can be your greatest ally in network marketing. Use it to keep in touch with your downline. Use it to call prospects and retail customers, because even if you're house-bound you can develop a great business with the telephone. Not only can you create a business, but you must continue to call all the aforementioned to keep your business alive.

Advertising, Newsletters and Mailing Lists

How to Write a Good Ad

Scary, huh? "What do I write, what do I say? Advertising may be way over my little pin-pointed head!"

When I wrote my first ad, I remember thinking how terrific it was:

**ATTENTION WOMEN! Own Your Own Life!
In the last ten months, working part-time
from my kitchen/office, I made $100,000.**
I am single with a child, and after a divorce had
struggled along below poverty level. We, as
women, are smart, courageous, and capable, yet
are generally relegated to earning sixty-five cents
on the dollar...I found a way out of that. I am
looking for women like you, to work with me. If
you want to help others and yourself, while making up to $6,000 per month, or more...Please call:
**Venus Andrecht (619) 788-0000——.
(Men welcome, too.)**

My phone rang on top of rings. Every woman in the county called me. Those without jobs, those who had never had jobs. Those without cars and with six kids under six years old called. Those who didn't know a health product from a gumdrop called, and those who couldn't, wouldn't, and didn't want to sell anything, called. Women with good intentions and no ambition rang to chat. One lady even stated that her religion didn't allow her to take supplements in any form, and she didn't believe in them, but maybe she could sell them? Women called with boyfriends who beat them, but maybe they could do MLM on the side?

And then the men called. "I'd like my wife to work. She doesn't want to, but this sounds good to me, could you call her?"

"My daughter needs to earn some money. Here's her phone number."

And, "All you need to do is front me $3,000 and I'll make you rich in this business."

Terrific ad. I never ran it again! However, it took four months for all the calls to peter out. I was thoroughly disgusted and wrung out. To cap it, I only got one decent manager out of the deal. You see, I hadn't been *specific* in what I wanted.

The next ad was well thought out and completely to the point. Under Business Opportunities, or Sales I put:

PERSON WITH MLM, sales, teaching, or managerial background, to introduce product which is breaking all sales records, internationally. Must be capable of handling exceptionally large incomes. Only those presently employed need apply. Call Ms. Andrecht (619) 788-0000 – Recorded message.

The kind of person I was looking for was clearly identified. It was much easier on all of us.

Specific Ads

These are ads that *identify* the product you're selling or the company you represent. For example:

> **DRINK UP!** America's drinking water is rotten. Call now for free sample of *Gummy's Pure Water from Hell.* You can have your own pipeline to sweet, spicy hot water in your own underground kitchen. Only $999.00 per month. Call 800-789-0000

> **YOUR HOBBY CAN MAKE YOU RICH!** Make great money selling fossilized fish-eye beads. Let me show you how. Hurry up and call Gil Salmon @ 815-000-0000

> **WANT TO MAKE MONEY OFF YOUR EXTRA FAT?** Lose that fat, fast. Looking for twelve people to join me on *Little Howard's Starvation Diet.* Make extra money during the time you would have been eating. Call quickly before I go into a coma. 714-388-0000

If you advertise that you'll teach people to string fish-eyes or starve, they'll say, "I'm not interested." Or they will be, but you'll more often than not have a retail customer for the products, not a distributor. With a *blind ad,* you get people who are looking for a business they can build, and that's what you want.

Blind Ads

Blind ads don't identify the product or the company. Peter's blind ad in the classified section went like this:

> **WORK SMARTER — NOT HARDER**
> Call Mrs. Robinson at (phone #)

Peter has told me that when he uses a woman's name he gets more calls. He thinks it's because most people don't feel threatened by a woman. When people call he answers, "Mrs. Robinson just stepped out. May I help you?"

However, a few days ago, I called Peter. He answered, "American Enterprises. Mrs. Robinson speaking." I was dumb-founded. He's become so brazen now, so sure of himself and his advertising ability, that he's passing himself off as Mrs. Robinson! I told him it wouldn't work.

An Exception

There's one kind of ad that works especially well. I've gotten many fabulous and appropriate people from ads for my counseling business. Other people have advertised their skills, too, and find it very profitable. Handymen, portrait painters, photographers, cooking and gardening teachers, and so forth, find it easy to spend time with people, doing what they've advertised while they subtly chew, drink, handle, or mention their products in front of their unsuspecting clients. What works here is that the prospects don't feel set up. In fact, they don't even know that they're at a presentation meeting and will, quite often, tumble into the net. What skills do you have? Use them.

How to Handle Ad Calls

The first time I ran an ad, I spent two or three weeks ruining every call. I didn't get one person to interview, but was exhausted from trying. I sat down and had a little chat with myself. "Now, Venus, don't cry about this. It's a learning experience. You're practicing. Yes, it's true that some big MLMers are masters at this. But they've practiced for years. You've only been doing this for three weeks."

I had been responding to ad calls the way the "professionals" had taught me, but it just wasn't working. Once I figured out my own style, it became easy. I suggest you do the same; practice different techniques until you find the one that you're comfortable with.

Once you have your response worked out, I suggest you get an answering machine or voice box, and record an introductory message about the opportunity, product, company, etc. Tell as much about your company and products as you want. Doing this serves several purposes: it saves your voice, it saves your time, and it weeds out people who aren't interested.

Spend some time calling other people's ads for ideas of what to put on your answering machine, and what not to. End your recorded message by asking people to leave their name, address, and phone number. Be delighted with those that just hang up; that's fewer uninterested or unsuitable people you need to speak to. Contact those who respond as promptly as you can.

Sometimes callers don't hear the beep that signals them to start talking, so be sure to put on the tape, "Wait for the tone." Otherwise, the caller may start talking too soon, and you could get a message like this: "...and call that number as soon as possible. It's urgent! I want to get to work right now and make you a million dollars!"

Hand-outs

You may have noticed little flyers stuck in car wind-shields, on walls, phone booths, and on benches (where you sit on them and they get stuck to your pants). They say something like: "STOP WALKING PAST A FORTUNE. IF YOU'RE NOT EARNING $50.00 PER HOUR, WE NEED TO TALK!" or, "EARN $10,000 A MONTH! CALL: 1-800-259——, 24-HR. RECORDING." Sometimes I call the number just to hear their hype, but usually these flyers don't interest me. One did, however. I was prancing back to my car after a day of shopping and, godzilla!

There was a folded $20.00 bill stuck in my door handle. Even though I'm pulling in a high income now, I still leapt on that money like I was smashing bugs! Inside, of course, was written something close to the examples mentioned above. The unique part that grabbed my attention was the $20.00 bill. It was, in reality, a clever copy — a real bill had been folded or cut in a certain way and then photocopied onto green paper.

Business Cards

Recently, I heard about a lady who buys one thousand business cards a month and then leaves them, literally, everywhere. I'm told that from sheer card volume alone she's doing very well.

John hands out his business card to any likely looking prospects. He wags his head and grins broadly while saying, "I'm looking for some real sharp people who want to make one to two thousand dollars a month. If you know of anyone, have them call me." He never asks them outright. He says this approach works on their minds. They have his card at home and it keeps bothering them until they call.

The Truth

How do *I* feel about advertising? I don't like it. It's not my style. It made me feel real busy, but frankly, I've only found two *almost decent* people from my ads: One still owes me money, and the other left town.

Two of my downline, Joe and Jimmy, advertised in a big, magnificent way. They got a dark, air-conditioned office with mile-high pile carpet and Art Deco decor. They began advertising in the newspaper, and soon had a number of people signed.

One man, Ed, was purchasing so many cases of product so quickly that we were all salivating with greed. Each of his upline (five levels worth) received $2,000 off him for the volume he purchased his first month in the business. The future rolled out bright, papered with greenback promise.

One thing puzzled us, however. None of the distributors who were so rapidly signing under him and ordering so many cases ever showed up at our business meetings. Also, Ed never asked any of us, his upline, to call or work with his group. He explained that he was busy giving home meetings and training his distributors *his* way.

We thought, "Well, O.K., it must be working, you can't argue with success." And, he *was* a charming fellow. He stopped being charming, however, when the district attorney's office let us know that our buddy had been busily using stolen credit cards to order all that product. He lost his last ounce of luster when we found that he had a long record behind him, and we just rolled over and kicked when we realized that we would each have $2,000 deducted from our company check the next month, when all that product was returned to the company.

Joe and Jimmy have since decided that advertising isn't

quite right for them after all, and are now concentrating on other areas.

Many people swear by advertising, but neither Joe, Jimmy, and I are one of them. It's one of those things you need to try for yourself and see if you like it.

Newsletters

Every week or two, I write and mail a newsletter to my distributors, my first-level (frontline) key people (they are usually my managers), the managers I've identified downline as key people, and others who need the information but have irresponsible sponsors. (I consider an irresponsible sponsor to be someone who fails to photocopy my newsletter and send it to their distributors; they usually haven't taught their distributors to do this either.)

This one item, a newsletter, does more to build and maintain my group then anything else I do. Along with my newsletter I also send flyers or newsletters from my company, upline, or other relevant sources. I suggest you immediately start to put information together and mail it to your people every week or so. Teach them to pass it on immediately to their downline.

What follows is a sample newsletter, full of eclectic bits of information.

THE NEWSLETTER

Dear Friends,   **Date: 0/0/00**

AN OPPORTUNITY AT MY FEET

Yesterday a friend and I were at Nordstrom's department store looking for shoes. For an hour we drove the patient young salesman to the brink of a breakdown. He had every red shoe on my foot, then every black one. When none worked he remembered others. We compared dye colors and found fault with leather, size, and fit. Finally, I looked at the fellow and said, "Why did you choose to do this work?" I honestly thought the guy would have to have a foot fetish to go through this kind of hell. (What I'm doing here is feeling a new person out, to see if he's a likely candidate for my MLM. Other questions I have asked someone are: Do you have kids? What do you do for a living? Have you ever thought of a career change? If their answers aren't right, I don't bother to do my song and dance number.)

My new friend grinned and said he'd just gotten out of college and needed a job while he tried to decide what to do with his life. (My ears stuck out and started rotating. Here's a likely candidate.)

"Maybe you'd be interested in what I do for a living," I said. "You're quite clever and charming." (A compliment helps before you launch your approach.) I continued, "I like the way you express yourself. You'd be excellent in my line of work. I'm always on the lookout for just the right few people to work with me in my business." (True. I want the best.)

At this point, Rob, the salesman, asked the expected question, "What do you do?" If he hadn't asked, most likely I would have dropped the issue. Rob wouldn't have appeared to have much curiosity or initiative.

"I don't do much anymore," I answered, "since I've gone from poverty to lots of money in two years with my business." (If I weren't at that point yet, I would have answered differently. Figure out, ahead of time, your answer to that question. You might begin by briefly mentioning the unique story behind your business or products.)

Next I said, "Rob, you have to come to a get-together with me. There's one tomorrow night for a few select people. I can bring one or two guests. I'd like to bring you." (If tomorrow wasn't good, I'd swing to another date.)

"Where do you live?" I ask, "Oh yeah? I'm going right by there. I'll pick you up." (Just to make sure he would arrive at the same time I did. Actually, to make sure he got there at all!) To cinch the deal, I pulled my beautiful daughter's picture out of my wallet and said, "She'll be there! Her last check was over $1,700." He can hardly wait to come, folks. He pleaded with me to let him bring his friends.

BETTER THAN WATCHING TV

There's a fellow who's done exceptionally well in the business. He started by tossing a company video on car seats with a note: "Watch the video and call me." He ended up with a line of people outside his house every night to see him. His wife helped out by serving them sandwiches.

DR. SEUSS AND ARNIE

Arnie was out playing "The Dangerous Game" the other night. This is when you go to another MLM group's meeting, just to check it out, get ideas, and look for new recruits. It's dangerous because you have to be so solid in your own MLM that no one can snooker you into theirs.

Arnie said that at this particular meeting, the leader stood up and read to them from the Dr. Seuss book, *Oh, The Places You'll Go!* Check it out. It's a scream the way it fits into the trials of building an MLM business.

INTERESTING SURVEY

The Mexican/American market in this country is largely untapped. A survey was done that says Hispanics spend millions on consumer goods and nobody seems to notice. Maybe we should.

THE RIGHT KIND OF PEOPLE

MLM research has shown that the ideal distributor is at least thirty years old, married, has two kids, two cars, a mortgage payment, and has an outgoing personality.

THOSE DARN DISTRIBUTORS

A few days ago, Sally called me, incredibly depressed. "Well," she said, "I'm pretty good at selling retail, but I have a heck of a time getting distributors, and when I do, they don't do anything. There must be something wrong with me! I just can't do this business."

"Wait a minute," I said, "Let me get my three-ring binder. This is where I keep all my distributors listed." I flipped it open to my most recent section. "Let me read you the last three pages. These go back a couple of months."

I started off with Hal who's in real estate and having a terrible time. "When I signed him, he said, 'Boy! Hot Golly! I'm gonna build this business. I'm desperate to do it.'

"Well," I told Sally, "it's been eight months and every time I see him, only about four times, he says, 'Boy! Hot Golly! I'm gonna build this business, I'm desperate!' He never does a thing.

"Then there's Sara. She was going to make me rich. Haven't seen her since.

"And Vince? He fell in love with a married woman and left to join a monastery of some kind.

"Bill and Alva started out with a bang. I thought I'd retire from what they would make for me. They got discouraged and quit.

"I finally got one couple who I think are really, truly going to do something in the business, and might even be 'super stars.' But that's it. One couple out of three pages of distributors."

Sally couldn't believe it. "Gee," she said, "you've made me feel great! I thought it was just me." And back to work she went.

My friends, I can't tell you how many people I prospect and how much time I spend, only to come up empty-handed. So what! The few who actually do something are making me, on average, $25,000 to $30,000 a month.

GET A MENTOR

Find someone to teach you the MLM ropes, someone who will help and inspire you. Ideally your sponsor or someone in your upline should do this. Other places to find words of wisdom are in books and tapes, by and about, present-day heroes like Buck Rogers, who built

IBM, Lee Iaccoca with Chrysler, Napoleon Hill, J.P. Getty, or Mary Kay, with Mary Kay Cosmetics.

You can find more in the bookstores and libraries. Look beyond them for historical figures who made their lives the way they willed and built them. Go to the biography and business sections of your library and bookstores.

TO STAY INSPIRED

Listen to the company videos and tapes as background music while you drive and work.

WHY WOULD YOU WANT TO DO MLM?

Studies show people get involved with a particular MLM for three reasons:
1. The people involved.
2. The financial opportunity.
3. The products.

THE BEST WAY TO BE SUCCESSFUL
IS TO SURROUND YOURSELF
WITH WINNERS...

...NOT WHINERS!

HOW'S YOUR DOWNLINE LOOK?

Your downline will copy you. Look at your downline and see how they're doing. That shows how *you* are running your business.

Pat accelerated her downline by getting product to them fast. "When I let my people say, 'Oh...I'll pick up a few boxes in a coupla' days,' I found my whole line poking along. When I hopped to and said, 'I'm coming right by your place in an hour (I made that up, of course) and I'll bring the stuff by,' my business increased tremendously. Everyone picked up the pace."

BIG COMPANY MEETING!
Get yourself and your downline signed up
for the big meeting in
Fleabite, Alabama,
June 23rd.
Call:_____

NEW COMPANY LITERATURE AVAILABLE
Five packs of 45 flyers with 52 print-outs and 15 response cards in five colors for $58.00. Available in five weeks, but order now because the company never prints enough.

VOICE BOXES
Remember to call the voice boxes every week for the latest breaking news, information, meetings, training and gossip. Get these numbers to all your downline. Venus: 619-788-0000. Martha: 213-476-0000.

Copy and get this to your downline immediately!

Thanks, talk to you soon.

Love,
Venus

You can type your newsletter just like any other letter. Or if you want to make a headline (and don't have a computer) get some paste-on letters at an office supply shop or an art store. Print your headline on some letter stock and just type in your information whenever you're ready to send out a letter. (If you want to get fancy, there's a good book called *How To Make Newsletters, Brochures & Other Good Stuff, Without A Computer* by Helen Gregory. The address is listed in the bibliography of MLM Magic.

A Mailing List

You need to have one of these if you're sending out a newsletter. Like I've mentioned before, get all the names and addresses together of your distributors, first-level managers, and so on. If you know how to put them on a computer, you're clever. Life will be easier for you, *maybe*.

If you use a typewriter, go to an office supply store. Tell the salesperson that you need to type up mailing labels and ask them to help you find what you need. Once you have a master typewritten list, you can use a copy machine to photocopy the list onto sticky labels that you can put on envelopes.

Of course, until your business explodes, you can write the addresses by hand. Remember to keep track of all changing addresses. Summer used to do the mailing list on the computer for me, but I forced myself to learn how to do it after she made a bad mistake one day. Somehow the computer managed to drop, lose, and erase everyone's first name. It kept one, however: Everyone on the print-out became Yasmin — Yasmin Jones, Yasmin Weaver, Yasmin Frank. Not everybody liked the name....

Mailing lists can cause problems. The worst time was when my computer ate the entire list. I couldn't find it anywhere! The whole business had disappeared into the innards of a humming beast! My mother had to drive down from the mountains to disembowel the computer and find the list for me. It took her five hours of frantic hunting before the creature spit it out.

Some people buy commercial mailing lists for prospecting. They create a special flyer or business opportunity newsletter to send to this often unwilling, uninterested, and unprepared group. A few of my distributors have had luck with this idea. I haven't. I think people are more willing to open a letter if they know it's coming, and if they know who is sending it. I have no qualms about sending my regular newsletter to prospects whom I've already met and forewarned, along with a copy of my most recent check!

Bulk Mail

If you have a mailing list of over two hundred people, you might want a bulk mail permit. At the time of this printing, it costs $75.00 to get the permit and $60.00 a year to use it. The cost per piece is $.198. Your bulk mail will have to be sorted by zip code, bundled, stickered, and sacked. This is a lot of work. The post office will help you the first time, if they're not too busy.

Will it pay to go to all this work and expense? Let's compare the difference between sending first class and sending bulk mail. It may not be cost effective. You need at least 200 names to get a permit, but if you only have 200 names and only mail once a year, it will be expensive.

At this printing, first class mail is $.29; bulk mail is $.198. So you need to do some figuring.

If you have 200 names on your mailing list and you only mail once a year, it will not be profitable to get a bulk mail permit:

$$200 \text{ Names} \times \$.29 = \$58.00$$
$$200 \text{ Names} \times \$.198 = \$39.60$$

$$\$58.00 - \$39.60 = \$18.40 \text{ Savings}$$

If you have 2000 names, you might consider it. Especially if you mail more frequently:

$$2000 \text{ Names} \times \$.29 = \$580.00$$
$$2000 \text{ Names} \times \$.198 = \$396.00$$

$$\$580.00 - \$369.00 = \$184.00$$

If you mail four times a year, multiply your savings by four to see if you will save money.

The more often you mail, the greater the savings, but, remember, it will cost $75.00 to get the permit and $60.00 for the current year. You can average the $75.00 over the life of your mailings, but the $60.00 is there every year.

To save any money at all on 200 names, you will have to mail a minimum of four times a year, and that's ignoring the $75.00 one-time fee.

If your mailing list is larger than 200 and/or you mail more often than four times a year, you can save money, but figure this out for yourself.

If you can get your message on a postcard, that's only $.19 per piece and no permits required.

I do my own newsletter labor because I like to know exactly what's going on in my business. I can keep track of and *edit* my business through my newsletter. This means that each time I send a newsletter I decide who to remove from or add onto my mailing list. I also decide what to write in the letter, and I even lick the stamps and put a short handwritten note on the outside of the envelope. Also, when I handle each letter, I fancy I'm putting successful thoughts on it. A big reason I do my own mailings is to protect the people on my list. I don't sell or trade my names. These people are my friends. I don't want to betray their trust.

Sending a newsletter is like being a cook. One time I made a terrific apple pie. I tried to duplicate it several days later when I was mad at someone. It turned out to be the worst pie I ever made or tried to eat. I'm sure my thoughts got mixed in that pie! If I hired someone to do my work, their thoughts might get mixed in my business, and I don't trust most people's thoughts.

Office Organization, Business Sense, and Money

My Beginning

My business started, and still is, on my kitchen table. But what a mess it used to be. I didn't realize that I was destined to make terrific money at this. This prompted me to treat my "office set-up" in a blasé fashion. That meant one small kitchen table and several empty shoe boxes. Very quickly that set-up turned into a paper tidal wave of misplaced important information and reduced me to a sticky ball of nerves and frustration.

The business soon progressed to piles of papers on the table, the floor, and the counters. Then the business spread through the living room and into my bedroom, almost like it was bugs with legs. I didn't like it in my bedroom. I couldn't rest or sleep, as my work, like a living creature, kept staring at me, begging me to come over and fiddle with it. Finally, a friend of mine couldn't stand the creeping intruder either, and so he organized me.

He got two cheap long tables and set them up nose to

nose in a corner of my dining room. On top of one table were two stacks of five plastic trays each. Each tray was labeled separately: Incoming Mail, Things To Do Now, Orders, Prospects, Venus' Junk Tray (eventually, there were 4 of those), and so forth. Next to this was another stack of trays that I used to hold flyers and company magazines. On the same table was my card file, some note pads, and several notebooks.

The second table held four bricks and a board that served as a shelf on top of the table. Here I kept brochures, videos, books, and a vase of fresh flowers.

On the walls were several bulletin boards crammed with important things I had to remember.

Under the tables I had plenty of things to kick: boxes for mailing product, packing materials, padded envelopes for mailing videos, and two short fat file cabinets on wheels. I still love those cabinets. They're open at the top with hanging files inside. I could hook a cabinet with my foot when I needed it, drag it out, and look right down at the mess inside.

And, of course, I had a telephone. For the first year I was working, I used Summer's old Princess rotary dial phone! (What a chore.) I made my first $100,000 using that antique!

Three-ring Binders

My desk was also covered with three-ring binders which I still have. One night, while giving a product and business class at my home, I was wowing people with the incredible amount of money I was making monthly. A man raised his hand, looked at me with a little eye-drag and asked, "Can you prove it?"

It had never occurred to me that some people might

think I was lying. The next day I ran out and bought a green three-ring binder (green for money) and filled it with plastic pages. Next, I took all the photocopies of my checks (absolutely, make photocopies of all the money your company sends you!) and slid them in the pages.

My checks from the company took about four to five months to start coming. The first one was a pitiful $12.00, but the second one was for $510.00. I yelled all the way from the mailbox. By the tenth month, they were up to $6,000 a month, interspersed with bonuses from $2,300 to $24,000! It looked good.

I added a neat notation: "This is all *my* money. None goes to pay downline. This money does not include retail money earned." (I was so excited by what I saw that I would have signed up all over again.) In a separate section of the binder, I put in copies of my upline's checks to prove I was no fluke.

A notebook like this encourages your prospects. They see the proof of what can be done by regular people and take heart. Before your checks start coming in, use your upline's checks. And there will be times when your checks will dip. Put those in, too. When your downline's checks are less than usual, they'll remember that this happens to you, too.

The next binder I bought was red (red for action). It is invaluable. I have it in sections:

Due — Those who owe me. Please. Don't have one of these. Be smarter than me. Make people pay up-front.
Distributors — Names, addresses, phone numbers. Also, whose leg they are in, and something personal about them. I mark down when I call them and what I send them. Anything pertinent should be noted.

Managers Under Me — This can easily get out of hand, so it's mainly people you have signed directly under you. Same information as with distributors.

Retail People — Names, addresses, phone numbers, dates, comments. I attempt to call these people in a timely fashion.

Potential Distributors or Prospects — Again, names, addresses, phone numbers and identifying information. Call them often. Send them copies of interesting company and product information, copies of your checks, a subscription to your company magazine, and so forth. Some people space their mailings out with something sent or given once a week. *Remember, you generally need to contact a person five different ways before you get a reaction from them...or catch the drift that they're seriously uninterested.*

Put the sections you call most often in plastic sheets. Trust me, you're going to think it's funny after a few years when you look through those sheets. Most of the people won't ever have signed, or if they did, they will have flown with the wind.

Miscellaneous Supplies

Keep all names, addresses, and phone numbers in a regular or rolling file box for quick reference.

Have some stickers made with your name, phone number, and address printed on them, and stick them on everything. Make sure they're stuck on all your products. As I've mentioned before, when people finish a bottle or box of whatever, they usually can't remember where they got it! And, of course, keep sticking them on little kids for a walking advertisement.

My Office Now

I've explained my original office set-up, and three years later, very little has changed. My office is still very simple. I now have a cordless phone which allows me to escape outside into the garden, and of course, I have an answering machine. In the garage I have a copy machine.

I did get a computer. Some people are pressing me to get a fax machine, but I don't like or understand the machines I already have, so why overwhelm myself?

I've also replaced some of those plastic trays with more decorative big straw chicken and duck baskets with lids. I just stuff everything in and put the lids on so I can't see the mess. I admit though, my four "junk" trays have progressed into a wire basket and a big cardboard box for the overflow.

I would suggest putting some kitchen-type cabinets up on the wall beside your work place. It frees up floor space and hides all your bulky product literature, videos, packing materials, stamps, stationery, extra folders and office supplies.

The point is, you don't need a fancy office, just a functional one, unless you have extra money you need to get rid of. I'm proof that you can work out of your home in a relaxed way and succeed.

Office Help

Get it if your need it, but if you're working out of your home, do you really need it?

I have a large international business and make incredible money, but I still answer my own phone and return messages, even though it may take days to do so.

I may not always be able to do this, but until my sanity is threatened, I will keep my own fingers on the pulse of my business. If you're getting really overwhelmed with your phone and paperwork, or travel frequently, or have little kids hanging on your pant bottoms, of course get help quickly. But! Before you jump, think, "Can I afford this? Will the office help absorb my profits? Will another person represent me as I'd like to be represented? Because whoever you hire will be *you* to those you deal with."

My brother Jim has a different philosophy. He's part owner of successful restaurant. He told me he never really started making money until he hired people.

Think, decide and choose carefully. The personal touch, *yours*, can go a long way toward building this kind of business. We're unique, you know.

Money and Business Sense

If you read my first book about MLM, you know I had a lot of trouble with money. When I had it, I tended to give it away!

Since my first venture into MLM, I got divorced. That act promoted more knowledge about money. My ex-husband insisted he had no assets, savings, or anything so we had to split *mine* between us, leaving my daughter and me to function in genteel poverty.

If I were to marry again, I'd get a prenuptial agreement, stating that I'm allowed to be generous, but whatever I make remains mine. It's not a bad idea. It's not optimistic either, of course. But man or woman, when you start making big money like you can in MLM, you suddenly become extremely attractive. Sometimes when my romantic life looks bleak, I tease about it and say, "Well, maybe I should pin a few of my big royalty and bonus checks on my chest to make myself more appealing!"

My Beginning Goals

When I started my present MLM business, Summer made a list of what she thought we needed and taped it to the refrigerator. These things, along with my own list, became some of the goals I worked for:

1. College for Summer
2. Bookshelves
3. Toaster oven
4. Waffle iron
5. New car for Mom
6. Our own house
7. Picnic basket with all the accompaniments

One Year Later, Here's How It Looked

1. College: After watching my accomplishments and meeting my company, Summer announced, "Mom, anyone who doesn't do this business is stupid." She immediately decided to work hard for two years, buy her life back and do whatever she wants (with lots of money behind her). At the moment, she goes to college, too, and is thinking of going into the literary and art fields.
2. Bookshelves: We now have some, but because buying books is our vice, we need more.
3. Toaster oven: Our old toaster oven caught fire, blew its glass front out and sailed across the kitchen. This happened while my cleaning lady's husband was making a melted cheese sandwich. Luis proceeded to scream and beat the toaster to death with his broom. We now have a new toaster oven, and for some reason my cleaning lady has a new husband.
4. Waffle iron: We've lost interest in waffles.
5. New car: I now have a new car, and so does Summer. Both are completely paid for.

6. New house: We now own two, one in the country, and one at the beach.

7. Picnic basket: Summer received that basket for Christmas. It has plates, silverware, fancy napkins, and long-stemmed wine glasses.

So much for genteel poverty!

Odd Thoughts

As you develop your business, to your disbelief and wonderment, you may notice that people have odd thoughts about money. One couple in my downline were starting to make decent money, at last. I met them on the street one day. "Hey," I said, "congratulations on your last check. What was it, about $1,500 for the month?"

"Yes," snapped the wife. "But what's the point? Most of it will go for taxes, so I think it's silly to make it!"

Several weeks later, I met her husband in the health food store. He said he wasn't interested in selling our product anymore. His friend, who knows *everything,* had convinced him that it destroyed people's DNA!

Then my friend remarked, "I can't believe I'm finding *you* — the Wine and Cheese Lady — in the health food store!" I just looked at him as he finished me off with, "Making all kinds of money now, huh, even though it's not a good product?"

"Got to go check the squashes," I said. Later, we passed in the parking lot, me in my new, paid for, bright yellow sports car and he in his battered, unpainted, window-shattered van. His mind tells him it's glorious to be noble and poor. Mine tells me it's glorious to be noble and prosperous. I guess we're both comfortable where we are.

Jealousy

A few words about people and jealousy. Don't be surprised if your friends and family attempt to hold you back from success. They'll try all different tricks. For example, with the couple I just mentioned, their *friend* convinced them to stay right where they are on the economic scale. I suspect that's exactly where he is.

I had a close friend for fifteen years. When she noticed how well I was doing, she began verbally attacking me in public places, telling me she was going to destroy me. Now, that's extreme, but be alert in your own life. People will want to keep you in your place.

You might feel guilty about leaving them, but let me tell you a story. One of my downline said his girlfriend had a dream. There had been a big shipwreck. Everyone was struggling, screaming, and flailing in the water. The girlfriend, Nancy, thought, "Oh, I have to save these people." She'd swim up to one and grab them. They, of course, would attempt to pull her under. She'd beat them off and swim to another. The same thing would happen. She'd try another. Suddenly, she heard a voice. "Swim away!" it commanded.

"I can't," Nancy thought, "I have to stay here with them."

"Swim away!" the voice repeated. Nancy rethought her position and began swimming. After several minutes, she paused and looked behind her. The screaming and thrashing had stopped. The people were watching her. Then she noticed a few began swimming to join her!

The moral here should be clear. Do what's best for you, and you'll inspire some folks to better themselves, too.

Credit Cards

Get a credit card. You can order your product with it, sell it all before the bill is due, and pay no interest. It's like using the bank's money for free. Plus, you have a tremendous incentive to move that stuff! That will build your business.

How do you get a credit card? What if banks are suspicious of you? (For good reason, maybe?) If you have trouble getting one, you will have to build up your credit.

Open up a bank account at the bank where you want to establish credit. Put some money in it. Make some sacrifices to do this. Borrow a little less than you have in the bank. You'll probably have to show your income tax return as well. Use the money in your bank account to pay back your loan (don't use it for anything else). When that loan is paid off, borrow a little more, and make payments on time. Add to your bank account also. It may take a while, but, once you've established your creditworthiness, you could end up with a credit card *and* money in the bank.

But be careful. Too many MLMers have stacked too much product and training materials on their cards and gone deeply into debt. Often they try to earn positions or trips by purchasing extraordinary amounts of product before they've found the customers to sell it all to. *Don't do this.* You don't need to look good in everyone's eyes or go to Bermuda with the company; you need to build your business and make money.

Taxes

Taxes are so boring and so maddening and so unrelentingly there. It's going to be a real shocker to you when you actually start paying the government more than you used to make in one year! That's what happened to me — the lady who lived at postdivorce poverty level.

Find a *Good* CPA Now!

You're going to need one. In the meantime:

1. Your car. Keep track of your business mileage. I keep a little book in my car. It has the date, the mileage, and where I went. Repairs, fees, parking, maintenance, and depreciation can be a good writeoff.

2. On the last day of the year, write down your inventory. How many cases, quarts, bottles, books, brooms, pots, cosmetics, etc., do you have on hand?

3. Label an 8-1/2"–by–11" manila envelope for every month. Put each month's receipts into the appropriate envelope. (Some people prefer to use an alphabetical system.)

4. Get a good-sized checkbook with carbon. The carbon tells you what you wrote when you forgot to write the check amount in the check register, and the big size prevents you from losing the whole thing.

5. Credit cards. Use them. You can order your product with them and sell the product before your interest is due. The bank is loaning you free money. It's easier to keep all your business on one card, and all your personal vices (purchases) on another.

6. File quarterly taxes. If you don't, and you've made some good money, your heart may short out when you find what you owe, lump sum, at tax time. Also, the government boys can penalize you for not filing quarterly. Whining, "But, gee, I didn't think I was really gonna make any money," doesn't help.

7. Find the right tax person. How? Take your chances, try a few out, interview, or be sneaky — you're always looking for super distributors, right? Find some of the best people in other MLMs (look in the yellow pages, go to other MLM meetings), call them and say, "You must have a really terrific tax person who understands MLM. I'm making such tremendous money (or, I'm close, I'm close!) with my MLM, that I need the name of someone really good. Can you help me out?" What you're hoping, of course, is that they'll beg you to tell them about your incredible company and then plead with you to let them sign up. You're still green if you actually believe that will happen, but you never know!

8. Keep a travel and entertainment log. If you want to visit Aunt Du in Hamcrack, Arkansas, write a letter of intent before you go. "Dear Aunt Du, I'll be coming back to Hamcrack in December. I'd like to show you an incredible opportunity..." This is proof to the IRS that you're not just running off to Arkansas for a vacation; that it's work that takes you there. When it comes to entertainment, keep track of who you wine and dine and take to sporting and cultural events. This means retail customers, prospective customers, associates, and prospective associates; in other words, just about everyone you know. In your log keep the date, name, the type of entertainment, what business was done and where, and the money spent.

9. Business gifts. Follow the same suggestions as in number 8. You have a maximum $25.00 per person, per year, as of this writing. Keep the receipts.

10. Home office deductions. You can write off a portion of your home, your insurance, gas and electric, etc.

11. You can pay a salary to your children if they're under 18 years of age.

12. Husband and wife can duplicate their tax writeoffs if they're both building the business.

Beyond this, taxes are still a puzzle to me. Find someone who knows more than I do...quickly.

Your Other Job

Don't quit your "real job" until you're making enough money in MLM to comfortably do so. Every time someone in my group calls me and happily yells, "I've just quit my job! I'm doing this full-time, now!" I think, *Oh no.* I know what stands ahead for both of us. At first, there is extreme joy and a sense of liberation, with great plans and much enthusiasm. As the weeks and months flip by, there are ups and downs, and then comes the Valley of Desperation. All the distributors they had pegged as having really "great potential" never came through. The contacts they thought were great movers and shakers decided not to join their group after all. The advertising that they thought was so super hasn't pulled in a single hard worker. Their family has deserted them, their credit cards are full, and the house payments are three months behind. They call me moaning and crying. I try to help, and usually end up saying, "For heaven's sake, get a job! You need the money and you need the contacts."

Multilevel takes a good while to build into something. The time to leap full body into the new life-style is when that happens, not before!

MLM Ethics, Problem Distributors... ...and More

One Week in MLM Life

Do you sometimes think you're the only one who suffers while building this business? Do you ask yourself after a tough week (or month or year), "Why the heck am I hanging onto this crazy dream?" To give your heart a little rest from all the grief MLM can engender, here's a typical week that happened fairly often as I built my business.

Vivian and Karen

Vivian and I liked each other right away. After we met we spent some time together, and later chatted on the phone a bit. I invited her to a big company meeting. She came and brought her friend, Karen. They both loved the event and product and gave me checks to sign them as distributors. The next day, Vivian called and told me they'd changed their minds. That was fine. Everyone has the right to back out. Then she announced that she and her friend were still signing up, but with someone else — someone they had met

at the big event —someone I had introduced them to —
someone who knew they were mine.

I was stunned. "Why?" I asked.

"I always do everything with my friend," she said, "and
Karen thinks these people can do more for us than you can."

"Do you always," I wondered, "do everything your
friend tells you to do—including stabbing me, your friend,
in the heart?"

As I thought that, Vivian turned the knife. "Karen has
always been very big in MLM and is going to build a huge
group."

An even bigger smack came later. Her new sponsor told
me that Vivian said she felt no affinity for me. I cried for
several hours about Vivian's careless remarks and callous
defection...then sulked around for another twenty-four.

Finally, I took myself in tow, as I suggest you do when
these things happen. I decided that I didn't want people in
my group who had no sense of honor, fairness, or friendship. I also felt that there was something weird about a
friendship where one person did whatever the other told her
to do. I predicted heavy fallout from that strange bonding,
onto whomever signed them up.

"Perhaps," I comforted myself, "I'm being protected
from future problems." Strangely enough, perhaps I was,
as that was the end of the story. Karen and Vivian quickly
dropped from sight, like two stones thrown into a river.

Good Things from Bad

From my hurt with Vivian and Karen came this realiza-
tion: First, I realized that I hadn't spent the time with Vivian
that she needed. I resolved to be more careful of that with
others. Second, while feeling shattered, I had called a
friend to comfort me. I hadn't spoken with this lady for

months. During the course of my complaining, I mentioned that I had been trying to find just the right house to buy for a long time, but with no luck. My friend said she knew where *The One* was, right in her own neighborhood. The sign had just gone up that morning!

The next day, I bought the house. It's just the one I had hoped to find. Who knows what good thing will happen next, thanks to Vivian?

Susan

The day after that trauma, Susan, a distributor who is a-ways down from me, called to scream about her upline, "Stupid Eddie!"

Eddie, she stormed, was a liar and a cheat, "And his brother is a deceitful, obnoxious pinhead!" It was something about a deal between them gone mean, and she was quitting the business and taking all her people with her to join another multilevel.

"You mean," I rephrased it, "because you're mad at 'Stupid Eddie' and his pin-headed brother, you're quitting this business? You're giving up *your* dreams, plans and goals and a business and product you love, because you're disappointed in *them*?"

"Yes!" she bellowed. "Good riddance!"

I silently said the same.

Eddie

When Eddie called, crying and moaning about how he he'd just lost the hottest person he had, I suggested he look at his part in the brawl.

I said, "Sit down and honestly ask yourself what you did that may have been rotten or out of line — and then vow you'll never do it again. Next, take a good look at Susan.

You're lucky she blew herself out of the game only a few months into the business. At this point, you've just been counting all the imaginary money you thought you'd make off her. What if, months from now, she showed her illogical, uncommitted self (as she was almost sure to do), and snatched $5,000 or $6,000 a month from you? You're lucky, Eddie."

"Oh," said Eddie, after a silence, "I didn't think of it that way. But you're probably right. She does get awfully mad about things."

"And Eddie," I said suspiciously, "what is this other MLM Susan referred to? Are you involved in it?"

"No, no!" Eddie rushed to explain. "Not me, Venus! I guess I'll have to tell you though. My downline, Troy, who signed Susan — he's also in some water distiller program. I've been really mad about what he's doing to his downline by confusing them with two MLMs, but I thought he'd wake up soon since his checks have dropped so badly."

"Uh huh, " I said. "You've put all your hopes and effort on him because he did so tremendously well at first, and so quickly. Wake up, Eddie. Let these people go. They're foolish, or at least immature in the MLM business. Once again, you've been counting imaginary money. Concentrate on the loyal, hard-working downline you do have. Try to save any good distributors in Troy and Susan's leg, and start looking again for new people who are smart enough to commit to *one* MLM and stick to it."

Take a lesson or two from Eddie's story. Every time something *bad* happens to you, stand back and look at it. Did you do anything to cause it? If so, what? Maybe you did a mean or greedy little thing? Or, you didn't see someone clearly? Or hoped too hard, or overlooked too much? Decide you won't do it that way again — that you'll be more aware. If you're sure you did nothing to cause the problem, then perhaps there's a positive reason for its occurrence. Watch and see what develops from its happening.

Mike

In the same week I've been discussing, Mike called me. "You remember Bert," he said, his voice dragging. "I've been talking to him about the business for a month now. I finally got him to come to a meeting, and do you know what he did? He signed up with a man from L.A., bought fifteen cartons of product, and went manager!"

"Michael" I soothed, "you don't want a man without loyalty in your group."

While I'm wiping Mike's tears, Lucy calls me on my other line and cries, "I only tried to help this woman and now she wants to sue me! I don't know why I'm in this business."

I promise I will call the lady and get things straightened out, but before I can get to it, the phone rings again. A man I've never heard of says he's in my downline and wants out. His roommate signed him up, and he's decided he doesn't want the guy to make any money off him. I ask him if he's spoken to his roommate about this. Well, no, he hasn't, but he's talked to the rest of his upline. In fact, he's managed to grab hold of all their feathers and outrage them. They all begin calling me.

These things happen. Not generally all in one week, but they happen.

Lucy

When I call Lucy back to calm her and tell her that the woman decided not to sue after all, I mention to her the week I've had.

"You mean," she says incredulously, "things like this happen to you, too, Venus?"

Of course, and they might even happen to you.

Cycles

The week I've just discussed was a bad one. Sometimes there are good weeks. Life runs in cycles, and so will your business. After several years of being beaten by business on the bad days, I've learned an important lesson.

Let's say that I get up in the morning and start making phone calls. Sometimes, three or four prospects or distributors will verbally batter me about their lives, their business, and their bad luck. The general run of people calling me will snivel and complain too.

Bingo, I think, it's one of those lousy time periods again. People are on a roll. It might last several more hours, or maybe a day, but I'm not going to subject myself to it. I hang up the phone and walk out the door. I know, absolutely, that every call will be negative this morning — because they're running in a cycle. I've learned to just put down the phone during these times and work on something else.

A cycle like this can show up in any situation; maybe I'm busy wrapping product to mail out, and after I've taped myself to the table several times, cut myself, and lost my rubber stamp, I think "Oh no, it's time to do something else."

Try not to get caught up in these cycles, or you'll end up becoming frustrated, grouchy, or feeling like a failure. Generally, I leave the house and do something fun, but sometimes I feel compelled to keep working, so I turn my attention to other areas and get busy. When enough time has gone by and I feel the cycle has passed, I go back to the original task.

Cycles also operate when lining up prospects and

signing distributors. I've noticed that people fall into categories according to when I signed or approached them. Perhaps every prospect I contacted around March 6th (or whatever date) worked diligently for a few weeks or months, and then quit in a puff of resignation. But two women who I approached on June 12th became managers and are adding $2,000 to my monthly check.

Recently, I've been working with eight distributors I signed over the last three months. They are all potential superstars. However, one by one, they've each come to utterly nothing, except for two of them. I signed these two ladies on the same day, and they have the same first name. Both are showing evidence of assuring me lifetime retirement.

Remember, your business won't stay in a cycle forever, whether good or bad. To maximize your chances, why not prospect, talk to, sign, train, and call as many people as possible. Throw them into the air like beans and see where they land. Some will hit the *right* cycles.

Stealing

Here's another little thing that causes problems. Don't steal another distributor or manager's people, even if those people beg you to.

Awhile back, a man came to me and wanted out of his line and into mine. I said, "No. That's not right. I know your sponsor, and she's a good lady. Ask her to work with you. Or go above her and ask her upline, or that upline's upline until you find someone in your group who will help you." He didn't. Instead, he went to another group, to some "big hustlers," and they gladly took him in, shaking his plump little hand all the way. Oddly enough, six months later, the guy isn't getting along with his new sponsors, either, while they find him to be a sticker between their toes.

Stealing isn't worth it. Don't do it. Your reputation and your feelings about yourself will suffer. When you start pulling slimy little things on people, they put bad thoughts on you that seem to grow and stretch and pass from one person's ear to another. Then, those thoughts and whispers trail you around forever and eventually wrap you in a negative net. MLM then becomes a horror instead of a delight.

MLM is much more than it appears. It's a chance to build your character How clean and clear will you build it?

Greed

Which brings us to greed, probably the main reason for stealing other people's people. MLM is a test. We're in a game, kids. A game that builds character...and exposes it.

There's a lot of money in MLM. What will you do, how far will you go, how much will you compromise yourself to make the most money? As I've said before (and maybe too many times), in my first ten months with my present company I made about $100,000, and came in as the second fastest growing business internationally in the company. I did it part-time and barefoot, while working in my kitchen office, mainly on the telephone. And I did it cleanly. I never knowingly or deliberately cheated or cut anyone else to get there. I can confidently say that most of my group is like this. Those that aren't like me aren't attracted to us in the first place, or if they are, they often end up just fading away.

You may be saying, "O.K., 'Goody-Two-Shoes,' that's fine for a little Pollyanna like you, but MLM is so competitive! If I ran my business totally fair and square, I wouldn't have a chance."

Listen — there's a bunch of people out there who will

kick and slice each other up to get where they want to be. Let them play with each other. Sure, lots of them will make money, but do you want to be like them? Do you want to play with them?

There are plenty of people like us. Play with us. Attract downline like yourself. Those of us who play cleanly will expand and teach, retrain and absorb those who haven't known any better. This is how my Pollyanna-self feels that goodness will take over the world.

And money? There's plenty of money. If a batch of us can play it straight (and most of my downline are just regular people, without business degrees or knowledge about high-finance or rough street-smarts) and make the kind of money we do, then you can, too.

Just don't be stupid. Nobody's telling you to be naive and let people take advantage of you. Stay alert. Protect yourself from those who don't know any better yet. And, when you're tempted to do something a little wormy because there's money in it, stop and ask yourself, "Will $10,000 gained be enough to paper over that clunky feeling that lurks in my stomach from what I did?" The $10,000 may disappear, but will that feeling? That thought? That sour reputation you bought?

Attitude Problems and How They Ruin Business

One day I encouraged my group to go to a training given by a man who had been in MLM for at least twenty years. He's excellent in multilevel; I think he's one of the best. The evening after the event, I got a frantic call from Frank, one of my struggling downline.

"Venus!" he wailed, "that man is too good. He's going to sign everyone before I even have a chance!" Frank was serious, and just in case you don't see the humor in this, let me explain. I believe there are at least 250 million people in the U.S. alone. Nobody is going to get all of them. Frank's attitude had dents in it. Instead of rejoicing at what this man had taught him, instead of racing out to apply his techniques, Frank burnt his energies out feeling jealous! For reasons similar to this, Frank eventually dropped out of the business.

Another fellow, Aaron, used to pout. He was annoyed because, "Other people are making big checks, and I'm not. It's not fair." Once, after a seminar where some big check earners spoke, I saw Aaron and his new distributor sitting in a restaurant. Aaron was pouting again. He sat, like a mean little five-year-old, totally ignoring his *baby* distributor, who, of course, was never seen again. Aaron begrudged other people their success, never stopping to consider that they deserved it, for whatever reasons. His attitude blocked his own forward motion.

Negativity and Rumors in, or About, Your Company

Sometimes a company deserves every bad thing you hear about it, but don't be too quick to judge. You could blow yourself out of a good future. Be a logical and cool detective. Many times, especially if you have a great MLM company, other companies and their people will start malevolent rumors about your product and company. They'd love to see you all go out of business.

Other times, there will be disgruntled people in your own group or other people's groups who will be quick to blame their failures on anything but themselves. Awhile back I got a letter, unsigned of course, from someone within our network who printed out twenty shocking "personal facts" about my company and our leaders. Some had a bit of truth, some were true, and some were total misconceptions. I got a laugh out of it because the true ones were more about people's characters, their human sides. The letter was obviously written by someone with a delicate ego so I tossed it. Nobody's bumping me off the track I'm on. I know where I'm going.

A few months ago a lady in my downline called me, wailing that other people were getting preferential treatment from the company. (So what?) She also complained that one of her downline didn't like one of the corporate heads. (So what?) Betty was wasting her creative time by thinking about junk. Some people get upset and feel ignored because certain people who are the favorites in the company (and there are always favorites) get all the limelight or are picked for choice assignments. (Again, so what!)

If this sounds like you, realize that your ego is getting in the way of the plans you have for your life. Let those other people do any kind of political dancing they choose.

Aren't you in network marketing to help other people and buy your own life back? Aren't you here to earn your freedom? Once you have money, you can paint yourself gold, lace nuts in your hair, and pay somebody to adore you. Until then, stay out of the company politics and competition. There are already too many applicants for those positions.

If someone in your downline has this problem, let them know, gently, that they have the choice to be concerned either about their standing in the company, or building their business. Which is more important to them — company glamour, or having a strong business with downline who respect them?

Negative People

As long as we're talking about negatives, we might as well toss in (or out?) a few negative people. To paraphrase Yogananda: *"Your environment is more important to your spiritual development than your heredity."* He meant that who you hang out with affects you a lot more than the traits you came in with.

If you want to succeed in MLM, stay away from negative people. Sure, you'll feel downcast sometimes, and so will your downline. That's normal. But you know the kind of people I mean. For example, I know a woman who is business death to anyone she attaches herself to. She's a lovely-seeming lady and she's interesting to talk to. She's interesting because she always has all the company dirt and scandal. She always knows the *worst* thing that's happening at the moment. You find yourself sucked into hour-long conversations, discussing all the gossip, the black happenings, the latest unsavory news. She suffers chronic depression about her own business. She knows *exactly* why it's not working: she's sure it's the fault of her company, her upline and the economy.

It's easy to fall in with her line of thinking, because we all have the same thoughts, at least periodically. It's all so familiar and warm. Beware. Everyone she whips into her web drops out of the business. Right now, she's having four-hour conversations with a man in my group who's happy to commiserate with her. He's a goner already. After talking to her one day, I realized how it happens. After that conversation, I felt awful. I was so unhappy with my company and business, I was ready to quit!

Then I shook myself and said, "For heaven's sake, you've got a great business. What's the matter with you?" Then, I realized that she was feeding off my energy and my rapt attention to her ideas. In every conversation we'd had she would take my strength, and then move on to some other unfortunate victim to feed elsewhere. We dummies kept her going.

People like her are called "psychic vampires." Often they appear to be regular, pleasant, helpful people, and in truth, they usually don't recognize what they're doing. They just seem to need us to live. Look at the people around you. Choose those who are good for you, and consider easing the others out. A few minutes ago, I got a call from a friend of mine. She was asking my advice about a woman who used to cause her no end of misery, simply by her presence and phone calls.

"Deanna has been hounding me for three days now," my friend said. "She left me alone for a long time, but now she's calling again. She calls me two, three, and four times a day, asking for my help on this and that, and pretending that she can't do anything by herself. I'm exhausted; I don't want to hurt her feelings, but I can't have her in my life anymore."

My suggestions were simple: "If you don't *feed* her, she'll starve and leave. If you keep *feeding* her help and information, she'll stay on your doorstep." My friend resolved right then to ease her out. "Every time she calls," I suggested, "be running out the door. Or be on the other telephone line, or say that your boss just walked in, or that your head is in the oven — *anything*! No matter what lure she holds out to grab you, run. Cut the fascinating gossip off before you fall into her trap. Be pleasant, kind, and warm, but put a stop to the energy drain. Cut off her blood supply."

Now, please, if people in your group tell you that they can't talk long, or often seem busy, don't automatically assume you're a "vampire." Ask them for a lunch date and make sure to tell them that you're serious about your business. You can also ask them if they feel like you're wasting their time or draining their energy.

Busy people often don't have much time, and when *you* cut all *your* vampires loose, you'll be busy with your successful business, too.

Some Don'ts

Here are a few loose *don'ts* that I want to mention, or reiterate:

1. Are you a rescuer? Do you like to save people from their follies? Do you like to snatch them out of their streets of poverty, their clouds of depression or aimless existence, their destructive habits, or ignorance? Do you have a knack for scooping emotionally mangled folk into your arms and carrying them until you drop? Are you tempted to save all these people and turn their lives around with the opportunities present in your multilevel? Go right ahead — they'll love all the attention and you'll feel needed, but your business won't grow a twit. You'll be too busy taking care of and encouraging people whose life work as victims gives meaning to the lives of rescuers.

2. Don't loan product or money to your prospects or downline. It looks as if I'm going to have to embarrass myself and be the example again. When I started my current business, I dramatically attempted to rescue most of San Diego County. I did it by loaning cases and cases of product to people who would, of course, pay me back as soon as they sold it. I loaned it, again of course, because they deserved it.

June was a lady I had just met. Such a sweet lady, too. She spent about three hours at my house. I heard about her younger husband who wasn't working but found the time to take out younger women. I heard about her wonderful son who wanted so badly to help his mama pay the bills, if only he could figure a way. The rent was overdue. They were soon to be kicked out. She was good at selling, but her current job just wasn't bringing in the money she needed. She just *knew* she'd be a whiz-bang at my multilevel. "Golly," she said, "if I only had the money to get started, I could make us rich!"

We worked a deal. (I realize now that the only part I played in this deal was that of sucker to a sensational con woman.) By the time she left, she had a distributor's kit worth $80.00, a case of product worth $400, and a check from me for $275.

You have to be reasonable here and understand that the money she earned from the product would pay me *my cost* for the case and kit (to be really nice, to help the poor woman, I'd let it go at my cost), and the $275 was to pay for an ad in a publication she worked for. The magazine wouldn't come out for several months, but in the meantime June could use the money towards her rent, see? It would work for both of us because when the ad came out, I'd be deluged with calls on my multilevel business. Somehow, I think you know that the ad never came out, I never saw a dime of my money, and I never saw (or could find) June again.

Now, I understand that the above example is outrageous and that *you'd* never do anything that dumb. Well O.K., how about a few more normal situations? You might be tempted, as I was, to loan product until your friend/distributor gets it sold — and then they'll pay you right back, right? People owe me approximately $6,000 because of my extreme generosity in that department. Some people actually paid me and the checks bounced, other people just disappeared with the product, and many are still leading me along. You may say, *Go after them and get the money!*, which is a lot easier to say than actually accomplish. It was a hard lesson, but I can honestly state now that nobody gets money or free product out of me. As lenient as I once was is as hard as I am now.

What I've told you here won't make a darn bit of difference in the way some of you do business, I know. People like us have to learn the hard way. But I just had to tell you anyway.

3. Don't wait until you know what you're doing to do the business. You might be dead by the time you get all your facts together. Just remember, no matter how little you know about your products and business, your prospects know even less.

My mother and I are like a little team in many ways, because we have something that we say to each other when we discover a new project, "Why should we wait until we know what we're doing before we do it? We'll just jump in and learn on the run."

4. Don't wait to do this business until you're out of college, your kids are in school, your husband leaves you, or France falls in the water. If you want to do something — then do it. The company you're enamored of will certainly not wait for you.

I remember a lady who couldn't contain herself at one of my company's big meetings She hopped up on stage, grabbed the microphone and said, "A year ago we were told about this business and we didn't listen. Then, we were told again — and then again. Finally, I got some interest, but my husband wouldn't *let* me do the program. I went along with him because I wanted peace in the family. Well, a few months later, he decided this was a good idea after all. So, we've been in the business about a month now, and it makes me so mad. I figure by putting it off, we lost at least $100,000!" She glared at her husband. So much for peace in the family.

Why Isn't My Business Growing?

Never let your ego get so big that you can't — or won't — go to every meeting, every class, and question every person about how they do their business. Even the person who is lowest on the pole (in your mind) may have a diamond of information that will change your life.

There was once a man in my downline, Rick, who constantly struggled along. I would invite him to company trainings. "Oh, I already know all that!" he would say to me. I would suggest books and tapes. "I read that stuff years ago," he'd answer. "In fact," he'd say, "I teach classes about making it in MLM." I'd give him a funny look, but he never seemed to catch on. He already knew everything he needed to know, and couldn't figure out why he wasn't succeeding.

In case you're like Rick, I'll spell it out: If your business isn't growing, then there's something you're not doing, or not doing right, and you need to find out what it is. So I repeat: Slap your ego and tie it to a chair. Then, humble as pie, talk to everyone...and listen. Go to every meeting and every class. Read every book and listen to every tape. Be willing to hear and do. Then put into practice what you are learning.

Another man, Paul, blew into our MLM group and announced that he was just the man to train all our people. His sponsors thought they had a "hot one" and let him loose on us, their downline. He thrived on running all our meetings and instructing us on how to make a million. Unfortunately, he didn't know much about the product, didn't have a downline, and couldn't get any company weekend training himself because those were his religious days. Well, he has a lot more time to pray now, because his business never happened. He and his ego preferred to dance on stage, instead of learning what he needed to know.

Another distributor I know, Donald, trumpets that he's failed at every business he's ever attempted. Now that he's in MLM, he states that everything he touches turns to gold. Only he's still making the same mistakes by leaving his downline to fend for themselves except when he steps in to snatch one of their possible distributors away from them. Success will be sour for him in the end. His downline only continues growing because they're onto a good thing in a particularly good MLM. If he were decent to his people, they'd break their buttons by expanding at a frantic rate.

Another reason that a group may not be growing is because you're cold and tight-fisted. You're so afraid that *someone else* will get and use your ideas that you're selfish with your bright thoughts and workable plans for business growth. You feel that if you place a good ad someone might steal it, right? If your wonderful newsletters or flyers get into another distributor's downline they'll take all the world's business away from you. If you're free with helpful advice and information, *someone else* will beat you out of all the wealth and glory. Unfortunately, these fearful, penurious thoughts make you and your business contract and grow cold. You feel so insecure that it's hard to be helpful. I understand that.

Personally, I grew up poor. The idea that "There is not enough for me" was so embedded in my mind that I had an awful time believing that I could be generous and still have plenty for me. I had to force myself to welcome people from other lines to my meetings and trainings. I *made* myself hand out my precious training flyers and newsletters, the ones packed with all my *secrets*.

Now, I write books that tell everyone how to do what I do! And I keep reminding myself that there are twenty eight million people in California alone, and I won't run out of contacts, and I won't starve. Doing these things works well for me. I've since learned that when I give you my information, you give me yours. The more I give you, the more you give me. Pretty soon, my group and I are so well trained that we're doing splendidly...and so are you. It's true. When you win, I win.

I now *want* to see other MLM lines do well. It delights me when someone else has good fortune, because my delight opens me up to what they have. You're destroying yourself when you feel jealous and small. Turn that energy around to applaud and support people, and your life will hook onto the magic upswing that comes with good thoughts, and success will be with you also.

Those Problem Distributors

In your distributor family you're always going to get some cuckoos. You might even be one yourself.

At one point, I was having a hard time dealing with a married couple in my organization. Everything they said rubbed my fur the wrong way. They seemed to speak eloquently and ethically, but their actions didn't match. I spent about a month frothing over their hypocrisy. Finally, one day, another distributor, Velma, was complaining about someone in her downline. "He does this, he says that, they aren't this...!" Suddenly, she stopped and swung her head to the side, "But, I guess," she said, "what I've been doing is judging him by my standards, not his!"

Velma the Sage snapped me right out of my misery and the complaints I had about my couple. Of course, they weren't hypocrites — they were just being true to *their* standards, which weren't mine at all. I dropped all the judgments. What a relief. I was able to get back to tending my own business — which needed tending.

The strange postscript to this story is that sometime later Velma called me and announced that I had done four things that were wrong, and she needed to set me clear. She then listed the four misdeeds that had completely "distorted, damaged, and undermined" our relationship and my character. The items she seriously dammed me for were so petty, nonsensical, and weird, that I was left in disbelief.

After I recovered from my shock and outrage, I had to laugh. Velma the Sage had forgotten her own advice: *Don't judge anyone else by your standards. They have their own.*

Isn't MLM wonderful? It's full of lessons and learning experiences. I mentioned this idea to someone in my downline the other day, after she had breathlessly related some tumultuous business flap downline. "Well, gee, Dixie, it'll just build your character," I soothed.

"Not mine," she snapped. "It's already built!"

I gave a little sneaky snicker, because by the time she's through with this business...if she can stick it...she'll have a character so built it could win beauty contests.

Frustrations

There is nothing more frustrating than dealing with distributors who have cracks and chasms cut in their thinking. With normal people, you can sit down and work out any upsets or misunderstandings that may arise. But with the other kind? It's impossible. Some of your most promising people will be unmanageable and unreasonable because of their wild emotional outbursts. One of my best managers, a lady who was leading all my legs in building a truly remarkable business, took offense at something she fancied I had done. No amount of explaining or facts could change her erratic thinking.

After a month, my daughter came to me and said, "Mother, I can't stand to see you so upset over this. You know you didn't do anything wrong. You've done everything you can to fix things. Just forget about it." And so I did.

Eventually, that wonderfully promising, extraordinary downline my lady was building fell apart. She has a million reasons why. I see only one: she wouldn't and couldn't listen to reason or think objectively.

Even at this very moment I have another exceptional woman in my downline who is in the midst of an emotional blowout about some fancied wrong perpetrated by her sponsor. Do I care? Not as much as I did the first time. Now I know to let these types go...quickly. They aren't worth the time you could be spending with more rational people.

There are a lot of ways to lose distributors, and I think we've mentioned most of them. Either they never do anything, fade away, or burn fast and hot, leaving a cinder behind. Some, as we've already mentioned, deliberately leave you, and it's usually a good thing if they do. Here's Heather's story:

Heather, a beautiful lady in her early forties, frantically called me one day. "After all the time," she sputtered, "after all the hours and days and weeks I've spent with Harry, training that man and pumping him up, consoling him and creating ideas to help him build his business...he's

...he's...Venus, he wants to switch sponsors! He wants to leave me and go to another group!" Her voice quivered with outrage, "The truth is, Venus, he's sweet on that other woman, Kayla! That's why he wants out. *She's* why he wants to switch. Well, I'm not going to sign him off! That's it. Period. He can just sit and rot in my group, not hers!"

I was silent for a few moments while I petted my cat. In these circumstances, I've learned to let my distributors exhaust themselves before I make a few sane suggestions.

"I'll tell you, Venus," Heather continued, "I'm tired of some of these people. In fact, I've been earnestly talking to the universe, asking that it cut loose the people from my group who shouldn't be with me, and to bring me new ones who should be. In fact, last week..." Heather's voice trailed into silence. Then, "My God, Venus, this flap with Harry all started right after I demanded that the universe clear out the laggards in my group! Oh my!" We both began laughing.

"Well" I said, " it looks as if you'd better cut him loose. He's always been an annoyance to you anyway. You've spent so much time with him and he's never lived up to his promise. Maybe he will with Kayla, but so what! Why should you keep suffering with him? Let Kayla suffer awhile." Heather laughed some more and agreed to let him find his own way.

A week later I got a triumphant call from Heather. "God works in wondrous ways!" she crowed. "Three days ago I signed up Mr. Perfect-for-this-Business! And he's already signed four people! He has come with me to every meeting, and we're going to a training together tonight. Thank goodness Harry left and made a spot for him!"

When you stop building your MLM with fear and desperation, you'll be able to let go of the distributors who drain you. You'll work then from security, the sure knowing that as you work, the "Big Power in the Sky" will help you team up with the right people for your group.

The Funny Side

Everything in MLM is funny. You just don't see it if you're looking from the dark side of the moon. I'm appreciative of the fun things in life. You can always find them tangled up in the mess that life can sometimes be. This morning I heard from Shari, a lady who dropped out of my group long ago. She was still a distributor, but completely inactive, and about five levels down from me.

"I'm ready to start all over again," she told me. "I think I can make it work this time." Then she rattled off all the reasons why it hadn't worked before, and how it was other people's fault that it hadn't, and how she'd been so good at signing people but they never stuck.

I interrupted to comment, "Well, you see Shari, that was the problem with that whole leg. Starting from the top, no one would listen to me. Your direct upline refused to let me train them. They wouldn't come to meetings, they wouldn't pass on my newsletters, they thought they knew how to run an MLM, and they didn't. You never got trained yourself, so it's no wonder you had the same problems they did."

"You're right!" she screamed. "You're right! That's what the problem was. I was just like them! I was unteachable. I never listened to you either!" I was startled. "I never heard a damn word you said!" she hollered. "I never went to your or the company's trainings either. I thought I knew it all! Happy days! I'm going to let you train me, right now!

I'll do anything you say. What should I do? Tell me everything."

I couldn't help laughing. I'd spent a year and a half sending her newsletters and calling her, and she'd never read or heard a word. I had probably even agonized over her, but I've agonized over so many, I can't recall if she was one of them. So much craziness goes on in MLM that you have to turn the tears to grins.

Start practicing now. Look for the funny side of everything that happens. Carry it over into your personal life; I do. For example, about a month ago, my daughter, Summer, almost died from a misdiagnosed ruptured appendix that went into gangrene and ulcers. Directly after the ensuing operation, I rushed to her bedside. Her dad (my ex-husband) was there also. The two of us hung over the bed, just watching her breathe.

Her poor father was so rattled and upset by this dead serious situation that when a new doctor (one of many) entered the room and introduced himself as Dr. Jones, Summer's father sprung upright and stuck out his hand.

With his head he nodded toward the bed, "I'm her sister," he solemnly announced. "No," he corrected, "I'm her son. No. No." He continued gamely, "I mean she's my mother." He paused a second to collect himself.

Sick as she was, Summer was shaking with silent laughter. "Oh God," I'm thinking, "and this doctor thinks *I'm* his wife!"

Still very serious, her father tried again, "I'm her daughter..."

"Never mind!" snapped the doctor, "I know who you are."

Your MLM will often seem dead serious to you, too. You'll feel like it's life or death. You'll be sure it's dying. Remember, look for the funny parts. A laugh is generally hidden in almost every desperate situation.

Three Areas in MLM

Once you reach a certain stage in networking, you'll realize that there are three basic areas where you'll spend much of your time. These areas are:

1. Building your business by finding and training new distributors.

2. Managing your group, which means keeping your people moving by attending meetings, sending out postcards, flyers, newsletters, making calls, counseling distributors, training new people to copy you, and providing help and information in other ways.

However, don't get hung up in the managing part of your business! Many of us begin by *building* our groups. We have to if we want to have a group! We make lists of people, call, write, talk, advertise, go to meetings, training sessions, comb the crowds, train the lucky folk who join us, and our business starts to pop. Then we get involved in *managing* — managing paperwork, managing our people, concentrating our hopes on a few good ones, talking on the phone a lot, and so forth.

We then forget to *build*. We become too comfortable managing. *Never, ever, get out of building!* If you find this happening to you, drop everything else and start looking for new people immediately.

3. Dying and Blaming. These problems are like two enormous sucking aphids on your MLM rosebush.

Dying refers to all the downline who dribble, drop, and drift away, which in turn causes you to blame them, the company, other people, and your products for your shrinking business.

Blaming is a total waste of time. You don't have time in this business to blame anyone but yourself if you aren't getting ahead. Take a good look at yourself. Maybe you already have the knowledge you need and just don't know it yet, or how to apply it.

Sometimes people groan to me, "I don't know how to get started in this business. I just don't know enough." These are often the same folk who are taking the products, going to meetings, reading the books and hanging out with me.

"For heaven's sake," I say, "you think you don't know enough to approach prospects? You know more about this business then *they* do. That gives you the edge right there!" And then I wallop them with, *"Someone* is going to introduce people to this unique opportunity. Why not you?"

Another cardinal rule of mine is: Don't be afraid to look stupid. I do it all the time, and it works well for me.

Do you think you aren't a polished business person? So what. Generally, the most successful MLM people I know are the most average in many ways. We don't scare people. And, once we've signed our prospects into the business, they often think, "Heck, if my sponsor can do this business, think how much better *I* can do it!"

Occasionally, some people will think they aren't getting off the ground or doing well because they don't have the right upline. They sometimes try to weasel and squeezle into a big name's group because they think their upline's success will rub off on them. Your upline *is* important, but if you find yourself in a dowdy group, it's unlikely that that's the main reason why you can't get started or don't succeed.

When I started in my current MLM, my upline was new

and didn't know any more than I did. We had to learn together. The person above them knew nothing at all, and the people above her were really too busy to hold my hand. But I had an inner desire to forge ahead and made it my goal to figure out how to do the business. *I* called upline for help. *I* found out about meetings and went to them. *I* collected flyers on the product, and *I* drove miles and miles to learn the business and become trained. *I* talked to people, *I* made the phone calls, and *I* refused to quit.

Nobody begged me to do the business, get training, or called to cheer me up. Nobody had to. My upline could have been no-account beanbrains. I didn't care. I didn't need anything but my own inner resources. Fortunately, I have a good upline, but I wouldn't have let a weak one stop me, or put a brake on my future.

What's the point of this chapter? We all have our days. Sometimes those days drag into weeks and months, but are you going to persist with this business or not? These situations and people give you a good excuse to fail — if you're looking for an excuse. Are you?

Discouraging Times
and
How to Cope

Depressions as Deep as the Sea

It's ten o'clock at night, and I shouldn't be working, but I've just talked to Tamara, one of my managers in a midwestern state. It's about 1:00 a.m. there, so I know she's in a desperate dip. She and her husband, Larry, have been steadfastly working this business for a year and a half. Their royalty check has never been one they wanted to photocopy and paste on their front door.

Tonight Tamara fell apart. She was having one of those really bad days that can often run into weeks and months. Tamara and Larry have never done MLM before, and they live in a part of the state that doesn't seem to leap at entrepreneurial opportunity. Both of them are hard workers and definitely not quitters. They've done almost everything I've suggested, and worked many of their own creations. So far, their ace hasn't come up. In fact, almost everything they've tried has melted into a sea of inertia.

Tamara is crying because all the people she's worked so

hard with and pinned hopes on spent the evening at home in front of their TV sets, eating ice cream and throwing peanuts at each other. This particular batch lives in another city where there was a big company meeting this evening — a meeting they'd all promised, faithfully, on their fat little honors, to attend. And that's not all Tamara is sad about: Everything she did today with the business came to a bad end. To frost her nickel, their tax man announced that they'd lost $4,000 on the business last year.

I tried to console her, "That's a great tax writeoff," Tam." Unfortunately, she doesn't need a tax writeoff. She needs money — money from this MLM.

"Both our families are watching to see how we do," she said. "We want to make good so badly, and we work so hard. What can we do?"

I always feel just awful in these situations. I empathize all the way. All I can do is play my "Salvation Army Lady" role and go in and save the dying. I do that by being truthful. MLM can be hell. It's often difficult. You get so many rejections. Until MLM succeeds, it's hard work and lots of it. What can keep you going is to realize you have lots of miserable company. Many people feel just like you do now. What makes the difference between you and them is that *most people quit.*

There's a short speech by Winston Churchill that I love. In fact, I have it taped over my work area:

"NEVER, NEVER, NEVER, NEVER GIVE UP!"

I tell Tamara this and then give her a dose of people in my group who are even more despondent, like Peggy. Today her teenaged daughter said she's quitting school, then put her fist through the kitchen wall when Peggy objected. Peggy said, "Well, if you think you're going to sit home all day and yak on my business phone you're badly mistaken."

The daughter sneered and snorted, "Right, and you make a big $600 a month off your silly business." Peggy has worked steadfastly, for a year and a half on that *silly* business. Things are just about to break for her, but that comment hurt worse than her hand after she smacked her daughter.

And then there's Adrienne. She worked night and day on her business and got it going so well she was making a decent $3,000 to $4,000 a month. Then her boyfriend began giving her trouble. He got engaged to another woman several states away and went to live with her. Adrienne pined and cried.

Then the boyfriend called and told her to get out of that ridiculous multilevel business. He told her that she'd never make it there. He told her to come to his area, that his new girlfriend could get her a job as a waitress in her restaurant. So Adrienne went! She's let her business completely fold while she sees the boyfriend when he has time, and works for the guy's fiancée.

I can only explain this by saying a stiff wind must have picked her up when we weren't looking, flipped her upside-down, and stuck her pointed head into the ground. When I hear from Adrienne (not often) she wonders why her business went flat and why her life doesn't work. Now, I tell Tamara she's a long way off from being in *that* bad a shape, which makes her laugh and feel a lot better.

I call the following tale, "No Rest For The Depressed." When Jackie signed with me she said, "Since my husband died a year ago, I've been very depressed. Sometimes I just take to my bed for a few days and can't get up. But I want to do this business. You may have to push me."

So I did. I'd hear that familiar voice in my head say, "Call Jackie. Talk to her. Make her get to work." So, I'd call.

Often Jackie wouldn't answer the phone. So I'd call again. And again. Eventually, she'd call me and admit to having been in a slump. She'd perk up for awhile, then go down again.

Ultimately I developed a harridan's personality. I specialized in berating her answering machine "Where's Jackie? What's she up to? Is she in bed again? Get out of that bed, Jackie!! GET OUT OF THAT BED. WE HAVE WORK TO DO!"

More often than not, Jackie would drag herself to the phone and admit that she'd been languishing in bed. Quite awhile went by, but finally Jackie built the business. The evening she accepted her manager's pin on stage at a company meeting she gave me some credit. "Every time I took to my bed, Venus would call. She harassed me so much that one day I just threw back the covers and shouted, 'All right! I might as well just get up and do this business. It's clear that Venus is *never* going to let me alone!'" We all got a laugh out of it.

Downline Depression Prevention

Never compare one of your downline to another one. You may be desperate to sing about how magnificent Princella is because she signed up the whole White House staff. Don't do it. Struggling Sally and Bloodthirsty Bill don't want to know how well their MLM cousin is doing...when they're not. Call your upline and brag, gloat, or whatever to them — they'll be glad to hear the news!

Never tell your downline who you've signed up, and how wonderfully the person is doing. It's a real temptation to do this. For example, you've just met and signed the top distributor of "Granny Grunts Pig Pies" into your multilevel. In three months you'll be so wealthy you won't even have to put on your own shoes. You're itching to tell someone. You need to crow and preen over your good fortune and business ability.

However, the majority of people you speak with everyday are your downline. You're so tempted...don't do it! Your downline will grin and congratulate you while bubbles of envy froth through their teeth. They'll slap your back heartily with forced goodwill while they think, "Shoot! Why did my upline find her? I never find anyone like that. Maybe I don't have what it takes. Maybe I don't know the right people. Maybe I should just forget this business. I work so hard to find good people, while my upline has it so easy..."

Again, because of human nature, it's best to call your upline, not your downline.

Burn-out

There were about one hundred people in the hotel meeting room. I'd just finished a wang-bang talk on how I built my MLM business, and how all the people in the room could do the same. Jeffrey, a man in my downline, had put together and run the whole event. As I watched him speaking to the group, closing the meeting with announcements, I thought, "How lucky I am to have Jeff in my group. He's so handsome and full of life, and he believes in what he's doing. What a joy he is." I reflected on how he and his wife had been actively building their group for three years and were solid in the business. After the show, I commented on his admirable handling of the event.

He thanked me. Then, suddenly, his eyes darted around the room, and he tugged me into an alcove. "Venus," he whispered, "I hate this business."

"What?" I stammered. I thought I had misheard him. "You said you ate the scissors?"

"No," he said shakily, "I'm going nuts. I don't want to do this business anymore. I'm so depressed I'm ready to cry."

He *was* ready to cry, and so was I. "Why? Why?" I stammered, again.

"Venus, we've been working this business for three years and I'm so ashamed. Our checks have never gone over $800 a month, if that. I'm so ashamed I could die. I get on stage and feel like a failure."

"Does your wife feel the same way?" I asked.

"God no," Jeffrey said, "she doesn't know *I* feel this way. And I don't want her to. She's so happy." He nodded toward Joanie in the center of the room, laughing and hugging and grinning like a jack-o-lantern.

"You're ashamed," I repeated, "because you're not making big checks yet? Jeff, you amaze me. You've never been in multilevel before, and you haven't found that magic one person yet. That's all. You've been practicing, learning the business. It's just a matter of time now, all the pieces are in place!"

Jeffrey rushed on, "I've worked so hard, Venus, around my real job, every day. Actually, night *and* day. I'm tired of it. Nothing's working."

Putting my hand in Jeffrey's, I said, "Jeff, you're *burned out*. Take a vacation from it. Pretend you quit the business and shut the door on it for two weeks. Then see how you feel."

Take This Business and Toss It — Temporarily

I knew only too well how Jeffrey felt. The day before I had felt the same way. Looking at a list of fifteen calls to return, people to see, mail to answer, piles of papers to be filed, and a newsletter to print, was too much for me. I gave it all a mental kick and slept two hours on the patio. When I got up, I had even less interest.

Then, unruly thoughts crept in: Will you ever want to do this business again? What if you have weeks and months of this, like you've had before? Should you push yourself to do the work, like you often do? Naw, my sensible self responded, you're frizzed out a bit. You need a mental rest. Put the guilt aside and go sit on the grass some more. You need reflecting time. So I rested.

The next morning I bounded out of bed, my mind pulsing with energy and ideas. I had just needed a rest. When this happens to you...take that rest.

You have to make a distinction, however, between "localized-pooped" and "long-term lazy." Treat them differently if you want to succeed. "Long-term lazy" may need therapy, or at least your willpower might need daily training by just doing the work. Pay attention and address the appropriate situation.

Maybe it seems a bit more serious, more than just being temporarily tired, or lazy. This type of thing happens in most marriages, including your union with MLM.

Yesterday, I was speaking with Allen, a fellow doing extremely well in our company. Suddenly he stated, "Gosh, Venus. I'm tired of people. I'm tired of doing meetings. I'm tired of this business. I'm tired. I just want to toss it all and go sit and fish somewhere."

I was happy to hear that and told him so. "I've been thinking it was only me," I said. "I just want to recline on my balcony and watch the birds fly."

We chatted on, stringing out all our disappointments, our exhaustion, and frustrations. At the end of a very fulfilling fifteen minutes, we hugged good-bye and bounded off to work, renewed and refreshed. If you love your company and your products and are being fairly treated by a good marketing plan, these spells will pass. Working all the time and eating cake all the time have the same effect. It can make you sick. Take some time off. Think about something else. After time apart, your MLM business, like your marriage, will look better.

P.S. Jeffrey recovered.

"I'm Tired of Selling, Hustling, and Hunting for New Blood!"

When this happens, readjust your attitude. Stop thinking that you're hustling, hunting, lassoing, working to find, feeling desperate to rope in, or otherwise snare new blood into your fledgling or flagging organization. When you're tired of it all, bored and disgusted and unwilling to pump or plop your product or MLM on one more person, sit down with a cup of tea and a biscuit.

Think how pleasant it would be to have a huge network of loving friends. How sweet to be able to call someone just to chat about feelings. How warm to be involved in bettering your community, or having fun with the local bowling team, or going to dinners for singles, or to cinemas with intellectuals. You could just relax, have a great time, get to know people, become friends, and just naturally introduce them to your line of work. You could even develop that network of caring over the phone starting with ads or cold-calls. Think about it: You may not be a cool-hearted hustler, a wild wheeler-dealer, or a fast-talking, fast-rising thunder-wonder like some MLMers. So what. People who are like you, of more moderate mien, often rise to the top in MLM like fine cream. And backed with persistence, practice, and a never-give-up attitude, you'll stay there...as long as you continue to *build your business*.

Your Family and Friends

If you're not discouraged on your own, your family and friends will be glad to help you out. We in MLM know that our families and friends are the first to say no to our products and our MLM opportunity. However, it certainly is amazing that we sell so much product! *Somebody's* families and friends are buying this stuff! You might consider making a deal with your downline; you sell to and sign up *their* family and buddies, and they'll do *yours*.

How to Work around and with the Family

In my first book on MLM, *The Outrageous Herb Lady*, my daughter, Summer, was about 7 years old, bright, and messy. She had, however, adjusted well to my business in our home. Picking up the story, Summer is twenty now, and pretty much developed. She is studying design, music, book publishing and herbology, among other things. Her room is still a jumble of sequins, paints, self-designed patterns, materials, musical equipment, flowers, pictures, old jewelry, and hats. She's a super achiever like her mom, and seems generally grateful that I'm home a lot, and most always have been.

I'm since divorced from the husband that trailed us through the last book, *The Herb Lady's Notebook*, and the last multilevel, and find that we're a lot happier! Mouser, my cat from *The Outrageous Herb Lady,* left for heaven at seventeen. We still miss her, but Big Tomi has pushed his hairy way into our hearts. He's a rude brute of a cat, but maybe that's his charm.

Working in multilevel with the family is easy now. We

cut a few loose, added a few, and all seem well adjusted.

But what about *your* family? Often in MLM, either the husband or the wife thinks the other has loose brains when the partner joins a multilevel. A lot of harassment can follow. What can you do about that?

Prove your spouse wrong. In my present MLM, quite often the wife gets involved first. The husband is generally patronizing or antagonistic.

However, as soon as the big checks start coming in, the husband says, "Move over, dear, I think you need some help." Then, of course, it becomes *his* business.

The couples who work together as a strong team are often quite successful. That teamwork is something to aim for: you do what you're best at, and have your partner do what's easiest for them. However...getting a couple to cooperate can be difficult.

Here's a little story about a couple in my downline. Sara is thirty-five and was very, very successful in the business world until she married Jon. Jon is her second husband, and is a successful and prominent man in his field. Once married, Sara had a baby and stayed home, thinking she was at least nominally happy with her new status. Then, she discovered us and our MLM. I remember the first night I met her and Jon, at an in-home dinner and business party. At the hors d'oeuvres table, she introduced both her sponsor, Julie, and me to her husband, and mentioned how much money we were making. Jon almost swallowed his olive whole. I thought right then, *Oh, oh. Here's a man whose ego is shaky, already. He has this smart-as-a-tack wife and he's scared to death she'll best him.* I could tell that it never entered his head that they could do this thing *together* and both rise to the top.

There must have been trouble in the marriage before,

because the simmer heated up after that evening. Jon took Sara's credit cards away so she couldn't order product. He refused to let her leave the house. He enforced that rule by taking her car away. He refused to baby-sit. When they went out with friends, he refused to let her talk. When she'd try to speak up, he'd cut her off. This and much more went on for about six months. Finally, she'd had enough and so had I.

"So how soon can you get rid of him?" I asked. Sara had already seen a lawyer and the leaving was in the works. The MLM was only the catalyst, of course, that shot Sara out of an extremely troubled marriage with an extremely troubled man.

If your marriage has more than a few problems, expect your new business to bring them to the surface. Most times you'll be able to deal with them and, hopefully, find peace and harmony by working toward a common goal...success in your multilevel.

When you can get your kids and spouse involved, do it. For example, give your kids a cut for finding distributors and retail people for you. When they're making money from your business, they'll support you. Where do kids find prospects? Most kids have teachers, and most teachers are excellent at multilevel...and need the added income. Kids belong to Little League and soccer teams. They go to parades and dance lessons. In other words, kids are people too, and they associate with other people. Who gets involved with MLM? People.

And your spouse? He or she also knows people. They can at least use your products in front of other people, wear them, or drop them into the conversation. What's in it for them? Maybe a new dress, a new car, a trip, or a new home? Maybe they just love you and what's in it for them is to see you happy!

Ask for your family's help and support. If they're antagonistic to you because you want to work in MLM, consider doing it anyway. Each of us comes into this life with *one* life and it's ours to live any way we choose. Why is it that so many people who already have one life think they can live ours too? Now that's selfish. Keep your life for yourself and do what you want with it!

"I'm Not Interested, I Don't Like MLM and I Don't Want To Sell. Disappear, Kid."

There's a magic sentence for all these occasions. It is, "I can understand that." A man in my present MLM teaches us the *feel, felt, found* technique.

"I can understand how you *feel*. I've *felt* the same way. But you know what I've *found?*"

Pull that tangle of words out of your pocket and drape them over your next negative prospect.

Encouraging Words

Remember what many old-time MLMers say: "It's impossible to fail at MLM unless:

1. Your company lets you down.
2. You're totally incompetent.
3. You quit too soon.

Most people think MLM will make them rich in a year or less. You have to realize that this is not a get rich quick deal. You have to work it and stay with it. Keep at it, keep at it, keep at it. It may not be one year, but two or three. Still, where else can you make enough to retire in three years? Or, who cares if it's five or seven years, just so you get there? If you have a good company the rest is up to you. Don't let yourself down.

Persistence

Jack, a man in my downline, told me a funny and true tale about persistence. Peter (a manager I mentioned earlier) got Jack's wife, Edna, involved in our MLM business. Jack said that was nice. She had a "little" business to work on, but he wanted no part of it. Peter thought otherwise. His plan was for both of them to take this seriously.

"As soon as he signed Edna," Jack said, "the calls started. Peter must have called every day to see how Edna was doing. Well, she wasn't feeling a thing from those products, but he kept calling.

"After three months of those calls, which always seemed to come during my favorite TV programs, I said, 'Peter, stop calling. I don't want to hear from you anymore.' Peter was real cheerful, Venus. He said 'O.K.' and hung up. The next day, *the very next day*, he called again." Jack continued. "I couldn't believe it. A few nights later, my buddies and I were gathered around the TV set. It was the big night, the Tyson/Spinks fight. We were all excited as you can imagine. We were hunched toward the set, hardly breathing as the fight started.

"The phone rang. I grabbed it real quick...and Venus, it was Peter! 'How ya' doin'?' he said. I yelled, 'For God's sake, Peter, I can't talk now!' All my friends started screaming and yelling; I turned around and Tyson had knocked Spinks cold! I'd missed the whole damn thing." Jack wiped his eyes and moaned. "Venus, only two seconds and I'd missed the fight of the decade because of Peter."

I must have looked stricken, because Jack quickly added, "Thank God Peter was persistent. A few days later Edna got the vision and became converted to the products and company. It's changed our lives, considerably."

Pep Talk for Discouraging Times

When we look at the biggest stars in our MLM business, we can feel pretty small. It is natural to compare ourselves to the biggest earners and come up feeling desperately inadequate. When this happens to me and people in my groups, I give us all a little truth-talk:

"How many of these successful people had downline groups to start with? It may have taken some time, but those who already had people who trusted them simply rolled them over into their new business. And how long have these stars been in MLM and/or sales? Often, at least twenty years. They've already spent their time suffering and learning and practicing the business. They're experienced in digging foundations for businesses, they've been to the "MLM and Sales College," sponsored by *life,* that we're now attending. They know the *right* people. They have contacts they've cultivated through the years.

When these people tell you, "Oh, this business is so easy and so much fun; all we do is lunch and sign people up," or, "Yep, I signed my second brain surgeon yesterday, and my airline pilot has the entire fleet in his group; what a piece of cake," what they're leaving out is the twenty years of tears and sweat that led up to these fun times. They're probably leaving out the years of heavy debt and bankruptcy, too, plus the seedy suits and peanut butter sandwiches they endured as they learned, by trial and error, their way to financial freedom. Don't let them fool you. If you have a good company and you study and work hard, believe totally in the goodness of your product and the rightness of what you're doing to help people, and NEVER give up, someday...and it may be a *soon* someday ...you'll be where they are.

But, I'll tell you what: there are always a few who make it on luck or good karma. Occasionally, out of a mass of distributors, a lucky person will get a distributor early in the game who makes him or her rich. George proudly told me he's failed at thirty-six businesses and four marriages. However, he finally hit the lucky card: He signed up a man who makes him $60,000 a month from royalties. Since signing this man, George has kept working, hustling, and signing other distributors, but after two and a half years, he only earns a minimal $4,000 a month off all of them. And that's *all* he'd be making now if he hadn't gotten so *lucky*.

I know a lady who just signed up *one* person. Then, she went back to her painting. That one person's group, at this writing, makes her $20,000 a month. As for my success, I had many, many ideas, many unique plans and tried them all while building my business. *Most didn't work.* However, the few that did got me where I am today.

So keep working, never stop. Congratulate yourself on everything you learn and do, and one day, you'll get *lucky,* too...one way or another.

Thinking Days

These are not a luxury. My thinking days yield more profit than a month of phone calls, classes, and paperwork. On "thinking days," I will often take a note pad and pencil and go sit in the sun. I do whatever seems right. Often I'll just stare up into the sky and let dreams drop into my head. Or I'll write up new goals and figure how I'm going to reach them. I might pay bills or plan how much money I want to make. Some days I listen to inspirational or teaching tapes.

I might scour my downline, thinking about every one of them, noticing how they're doing, who's needing help, who I should be neglecting because they've neglected the business, who I should be paying more attention to because they're working so hard, or doing so well.

Here's something I do that I believe has a lot to do with making my business grow: I don't know why this is, but in my heart, right in the center of myself, I round up all these people and love them. I want them to succeed. I want them to build respect for themselves as they build the business. When I look at them individually, I fancy that I can see what holds them back, where their strong points are, and their weaker areas too. I think real hard about them overcoming and pushing upward. I picture them doing as well as me, and even passing me up. Then, I think about all the other lines in the company. These are people who aren't in my group, hence, I make no money off them, but I find that I want them to succeed also! They're like a pack of cousins, and I want us to all be at the same party. Then, odd as it seems, that circle I'm thinking of expands to include all the people of the world, and I find myself wishing them all harmony, grace, and prosperity.

These thoughts and feelings are with me every day. I don't make them be there. They just come. I feel I'm swept up in a spiral of goodwill and positivism...and the only direction for all of us is u*p*. If I were to spend time feeling jealous over another's success or wishing someone ill luck or misfortune so that I might shine more brightly, I feel I would drop from the spiral. So, whenever those common thoughts pierce me, I give them a smack and give myself a stern lecture. Truly, truly, if you wish harm for others, you will inherit the harm yourself. If you don't wish harm but are only out for yourself, and perhaps a few close friends and family, any success you have will be laced with an empty feeling. That can happen when you're standing on the broken backs of others, even if you broke them only with your thoughts.

Plan, Build, and
Keep Yourself Sane

What MLM Really Is

When MLM is practiced successfully, it is a life game that teaches us how to expand ourselves and help humankind.

1. We begin by helping three to five frontline people learn how to build a business and prosper by helping downline.

2. We help them even further by helping those under them, and those under them, and even deeper.

3. We do this by putting on meetings for our downline, often leaving the warmth of our home and traveling long distances.

4. We call our people on the phone.

5. We inspire them.

6. We send them Christmas cards. And tapes. And books.

7. We write informational flyers, just for them.

8. We are a friend indeed, a lifter in times of discouragement.

9. They are always on our minds as we ask ourselves, "What can I do to help them build their business and earn their financial freedom?"

As our enforced generosity extends itself, our security fears drop away and our light and true generosity shines through. Soon, we want to help our family (the people of the world) to have what we have, materially and spiritually. We want to pull them upwards, along with us, into happiness and prosperity, because what fun is it to be there alone?

After you've been in MLM awhile and played the game in a clean way (without being naive or foolish!), look back at your former self. Now see if you aren't a bit more pure, more noble, more open-hearted, and loving now than you used to be. I'll bet you are! I'll bet you're riding closer to sainthood than you've ever been!

On Those "Nothing-Happening" Days (or Weeks)

There will be bleak periods in your business when nothing seems to be happening at all. Following are a few thoughts and suggestions that may motivate you to turn that depressing *downtime* into inspiring and business-building *uptime*.

Positive Moves

The sky is gray and hung with mist today. The pots of flowers I'd hoped to plant sit on my porch, weak with disinterest. I feel the same. Inside, the phone doesn't ring. I've cleaned the cat box, punched the couch pillows and rubbed dust off the sideboards.

Now my office and business call to me. The phone that isn't ringing is the one that has replaced Summer's old Princess dial phone. It's now *Sheila,* the phone who does everything. She accurately logs calls, then remarks on the date and time. I can turn off her ring, and turn off her messages, but there's one thing I can't do — shut Sheila up. After every call, she announces in a strident voice, "The time is! 4:45 p.m.!" or whatever. Today she's stubbornly silent. I sit down at my table. It's a mess.

A quiet day is a day to clean...and sometimes I do, but more often I don't, since I've learned instead to use these slack times for a multitude of things.

• Often I call downline I've neglected.
• Make file cards on people.
• Ideas are collected and written up for my newsletter.
• Sometimes I deposit money.
• Pay bills.
• Send information.
• Make calls to potential distributors.
• Many times I write up my goals and how I'm going to get there.
• But, mostly I think, long, hard, and creatively, as I've already mentioned under Thinking Days.

But let me expand even more on this idea. Thoughts, to me, are a moving substance. When I work with them it's almost like stacking blocks.

I picture my ideas building my business. That old saying is so true: "Everything in existence today was once a thought...a daydream." The days I spend daydreaming bring more concrete results than thirty days of physical activity. I recommend that you give up feeling gloomy during your seemingly unproductive times, and specialize in thinking your business into a booming enterprise.

Visualizing And Writing A Plan

Kathryn visualizes herself on stage accepting awards from her MLM company. In her mind, she continually runs to her mailbox where she finds enormous royalty checks, while she keeps the phone in her head always ringing with new, active distributors.

When I was in real estate, I used to spend time every day visualizing myself depositing stacks of checks and cash. It came to pass, not with real estate, but with my MLM business.

Often, I'll saunter down to the beach and sit for hours with a pad and pencil. Here's what I came up with January first, a year after I'd started my present business:

Page 1: Listed all my bills, including those for the business. On the same page, I wrote down the amount of money I needed to pay off an acre of land, the amounts I wanted for savings, needed for taxes, hoped to have for investments, and had to have for living expenses.

Page 2: Penciled out the amount I needed to earn every month to do the above. That became my goal. I needed to make a certain royalty check each month from my MLM business. In big letters I wrote, "GOAL: $15,000, or more, a month royalty!" Then I figured out and wrote down how many working legs I needed, how much they should average a month for me to make that kind of money: "EIGHT LEGS making $2,000 or more per month."

Page 3: Contained all the steps I'd need to follow that year to reach, and hopefully surpass, my goals. Page 3 turned into three pages, covered back and front. I called it:

Ideas to Build My MLM Business This Year

Training

1. Teach my people how to build their business this year.

2. With each new distributor, I train them on the spot, or at a weekly meeting. Have a business meeting every Tuesday for new distributors, old ones, managers, etc.

3. Get people to local company meetings. I must go, too. All of us must go to at least one meeting a week. Try going to the meetings in all the surrounding cities to learn different things.

4. Teach new people, when they first start this business, that it's important to go to a meeting every day. I show them my appointment book for last year, when I first started. Point out that it's empty in January and part of February, except for meetings every night. I'd often go alone.

5. Work hard with those who are serious. Let the others drop away.

Planning

1. Write down all my ideas for business building. Be creative and wild.

2. Write out the kinds of people I want in my business:

    a. Entrepreneurial women. Of all the people involved in MLM, 85% are women. Many women are leaving the corporate world for an in-home job.

    b. Couples. Look for those who have just retired and still may want to work.

    c. People with backgrounds in life insurance, sales, teaching, managerial, or service jobs.

    d. People tired of just slogging along in life.

    e. People with enough money to start this business.

    f. Hard-working, persistent, honorable people.

3. Keep thinking up new approaches to this business. If one doesn't work (or five or six!), try others.

4. Ask my people, "How well do you want to succeed in this business? If you futz around and find that everything else takes your time, you'll always stay right in the lifestyle you're at now. This business won't wait for you."

Working with & for My Group

1. Get flyers and newsletters to all my downline. Teach them to do the same, and check to see that they do.

2. Work consistently with those who show me they mean business. I want to see action and results, and I'm here to help people make that happen. Those who call me get my attention. However, keep in touch with the others. Some resurrect themselves.

Educate Self & Group

1. Take one day a week, or an hour or two a day, to think and plan and visualize my success. Take Sundays and spend hours writing my plans, reviewing old ones, and *seeing* the results in my mind. Put power and enjoyment into it.

2. Buy more MLM books and tapes. Encourage my downline to do the same, and have them get the material to their downline.

3. Two out of every five of my frontline need to be three levels deep. I can then let those two go on their own a bit while I get two more frontline three levels deep.

4. Idea: Take one of my downline and go out to lunch where there are people. The two of us can then start talking excitedly about our wonderful product. Strangers around us may be curious and ask questions. If not, we've had a *writeoff* lunch and a jolly time.

Care of New Distributors

1. After signing a new distributor, ask them to read all materials and listen to and watch our tapes and videos. Set a date for them to train with me a few days later. If they haven't done the work by then, consider how much time I should realistically spend with them.

2. Make a list of what my new distributors need at time of sign-up.

3. Treat my new people as if they are *babies* for at least thirty days, because they are. Give them a chance to show if they're serious. If not, don't waste my time. Look for new ones. There are 250 million people in the U.S. While going through the numbers, think about how many people a person has to date before they find the right one, or get married. (Business odds are quite a bit better!)

Take Care of Business

1. Order more products and supplies. I can't sell from an empty wagon.

2. Get a copy machine.

3. Get a business checkbook.

4. Advertise in the local business journal.

5. Figure a way to get write-ups on myself in local newspapers, so I'll get business inquires.

6. Get a gas credit card for business expenses.

7. Get a MasterCard or Visa to keep track of other business expenses. Pay it off at the end of each month, or it can become a monster.

8. Have a board on my wall listing all my best people with phone numbers, and all my future managers (even if they don't recognize it) with phone numbers.

Personal Encouragement

1. Never Give Up — Make It Happen.

2. Make a new list detailing why I'm building this business and tack it over my desk to encourage me to keep going.

3. Put a message on my voice box: "What are your goals for the new year? Do you plan to make this business happen? Will you be undaunted and courageous? Are you able to say "next" and move on?"

Keep in Touch

1. Call the Andersons about them making manager in time to be at the convention.

2. Work especially with Deanne's group. It has some good lines, but needs my help.

3. Work three to four or even eight to ten or more levels deep, whatever it takes, to find the jewels.

4. Do weekly trainings on my voice box.

5. *Copy and get these pages to all my downline to help them plan their new year's business.*

Can you make the time, right now, to take some thinking hours, or the entire day to create? Here's the space to make plans for your new year in MLM, no matter what month and date it is today. Start by figuring your monthly financial needs.

On the following page is a short form, "What I Need to Earn Monthly This Year, and Why," designed to help you determine what your starting goals in MLM should be. Take a few minutes to think about your answers as you fill in the blanks. The time you spend now will help you chart a direct course for the new year in MLM.

What I Need to Earn Monthly This Year, and Why

1. Bills I owe monthly, including monies needed to run this business: $_____.

2. Amount needed to pay off car, land, credit cards, etc. (if this is your plan): $_____.

3. Amount needed for savings, investments, and taxes, for this year: $_____.

4. Any other money needed: $_____ and for what:_____.

5. The amount I need to earn monthly to cover **all** the above: $_____. (You can include in this amount what you already earn at your "real job," or figure the amount you need to earn solely from your MLM.) Write down the amount you need to earn.

6. The amount I need to earn each month from my MLM: $_____.

7. This is my goal: $_____ or more per month. (Write it big and bold, so it sinks in!)

Now, turn to the next section, "Ideas to Build My MLM Business This Year," and creatively fill it out. Get a separate sheet of paper, if you need it. Remember, the more ideas you have, the more you have to work with.

Ideas to Build My MLM Business This Year

In order to make $_____ per month:

Training

1. _____
2. _____
3. _____
4. _____

Planning

1. _____
2. _____
3. _____
4. _____

Working with & for My Group

1. _____
2. _____
3. _____
4. _____

Educate Self & Group

1. _____
2. _____
3. _____
4. _____

Care of New Distributors

1. _____
2. _____
3. _____
4. _____

Take Care of Business

1. _____
2. _____
3. _____
4. _____

Personal Encouragement

1. _____
2. _____
3. _____
4. _____

Keep In Touch

1. _____
2. _____
3. _____
4. _____
5. *Copy and get these pages to all my downline to help them plan their new year's business.*

Your Physical & Mental Health and Other People's Rules

In my old life (when I was married and in another MLM) I thought I had to live by other people's rules. People would call me at any hour of the day or night...and I would answer.

You don't have to answer a phone just because it rings; did you know that? Now I have an answering machine. When I don't want to talk, I flat don't. Sometimes I even let it ring, listen to the message, then call them right back. It just gives me a feeling of power — power over my own life.

In my old life, I even allowed people to show up at my door anytime they chose. I'd often be working with people from the time the sun came up, until late at night.

Once, I'd had an especially heavy day and was exhausted. One of my downline called at 11:00 p.m.— she wanted to come over and get some help. I dared to say I really couldn't; it was too late and I was tired.

My then-husband jumped in with, "How can you be so selfish! Tell her to come over. She needs your help." Well, you see, the nerve-tearing pace of my work life, which was killing *me*, was supporting *him*.... It took me many years to realize who was truly selfish.

Awhile back, before I learned to demand my early morning think-and-be-peaceful time, the phone rang. I was still asleep, and so I shot up in bed like a loose spring. It was Beth, a lady I'd met a few weeks before. She'd been using one of my products, and chatted on agreeably about it as I nosed my way up from a semiconscious state. She casually mentioned she'd been home from work for two days with a headache.

"Oh, that's probably the product," I reminded her. "Remember, I told you that might happen while it pulled some toxins out of your body. To stop the headaches," I volunteered, "just—."

"Whaaat?!" Beth screeched. "You mean I've missed two days of work because of you?! I can't afford to miss work. This is outrageous!" she stormed. "What kind of person are you?! I've had enough of you!" She slammed down the phone.

Thank goodness, because I'd had enough of her, too. Shaking now, I was back to life, wide awake and ready for the day — and what a day. Throughout its entirety, Beth's voice careened through my head. Everything I attempted to do was colored and permeated by the imprint she'd left on my early-morning, open mind. A lost day in hell was what I had.

It's very important how you wake up in the morning. You're wide open to all suggestions and influences. My recommendation is to use this impressionable time to better your life. That's why I listen to classical music and read spiritually enhancing books. It's probably an excellent time to listen to positive tapes, or tapes relating to your business.

Be selfish with your life. If you're panicked, over-worked, worried and wild, both you and the work suffer. Take a break. Take time off. Set hours and rules for yourself. People will take as much advantage of you as you let them. When you're finally a millionaire, do you want to be an empty shell? I've known a few people who ruined their minds and health to get where they wanted to be. At that point, they were either so sick or dead that their kids or private nurses had all the fun with the money.

Ride Your Own Horse

Today, I had a nice conversation with "Happy Henry." You remember: he's the seventy-five-year-old fellow who signed me into my first multilevel. (You may have met him in the first chapter of my first book, *The Outrageous Herb Lady...How to Make a Mint in MLM.*) He was advising me to take it easy — to relax and not work so hard.

I said, "Henry, you remember me from before, but now I sometimes feel like I hardly work anymore. Life is slipping by too quickly for me to miss any more spring-times, sunsets, and time with friends."

We talked about various multilevels and how, even when we're making good money, many of them have a velvet whip at our backs. They're always thinking up new ways to keep us competing with each other within the company. We're constantly being pushed to do more, work harder, make more money, qualify for prestigious trips, cars, bonuses and advanced positions. Our egos are manipulated. We're made to feel unable and somehow inferior if we don't keep up the pace the company sets. We may feel lacking as leaders, that we're not as good as others, and are falling behind. We may indeed have positions within the company and feel pressured to keep up, to do more, strive harder and progress farther. Some people love and thrive on this, while others find it stressful and upsetting.

My advice to you is to ride your own horse and follow your own flag. Set *your* goals and follow them. There's no need for you to follow someone else's goals just because they tell you to! Don't get sucked in by all the glory, glamour, and ego pumping. It's a GAME, kids. Do you want to play it? If it's good for your physical and mental health, join in. If not, reconsider. What do you care about all the company fru-fru if you're getting to the goals you've set, the ones that are right for you?

Another Mind-saving Device:
Hired Help

As soon as you can afford it, get someone to clean your house — or at least to stack your papers and squash the ants in the kitchen. You're busy earning your freedom, and you can use a little help.

My latest helpers are Maria and her new husband, Ramon. (Remember, her former husband disappeared after the toaster blew up and shot across the room.) Maria is a sweet, short, round-sided lady with cropped spiky hair and several silver teeth. Ramon looks like a Greek god and adores fat Maria.

A terrible thing happened to them last week when they attempted to clean my house. Maria breathlessly reported the following events to me on the phone that evening. They had just come in the door and started to work when my security system went off. This is no ordinary system: There is a horn the size of an orange crate and a siren that sounds like the true hounds of hell.

Ramon leapt into action and attempted to cover the horn with rags. Then he tried pillows. The parakeets were hopping and screeching, while Tomi, our cat, frantically pawed open a kitchen cupboard, slithered in, and pulled the door after him. No regular person could stay in the house with that racket; it's set to scare the red devil out of intruders and shake their brains.

But Maria and Ramon? They were there to work, and work they did. Maria proceeded to race through the dishes as Ramon furiously dusted.

"Suddenly," Maria told me, "the front door flew open and three policemen ran in, pointing their guns at us." She paused to breathe. "We dropped everything and threw our arms in the air," Maria said. "We were scared." (Maria is a marvel of understatement.) "They yelled at us and asked what we were doing!"

Apparently Maria looked like she was making off with my dishes and Ramon was handling the furniture removal. After a search and heavy questioning, the two were able to prove their innocence, but it didn't stop there: the siren was still screaming when the fire trucks came.

Half an hour later, with the help of three policemen and five firemen, the siren was turned off. Peace returned. Maria and Ramon went shakily back to their cleaning.

"Then," said Maria, "I opened the front door. The siren went off again, Venus! This time," she sighed, "Ramon and I knew what would happen. We just walked out front and waited."

P.S. Maria had forgotten the security code, but I'll bet she never will again. There's nothing like a good trauma to indent your mind and impress your memory.

P.P.S. You may remember my incredible housecleaner, Josie, from my book, *The Outrageous Herb Lady*. In case you're worried about her, she was replaced only because we moved to another town. Otherwise, she'd be with me still, busily drinking my cleaning powders and liquor.

Will You Make It in MLM?

Summing Up

One of my ladies, Sybyl, came to visit me the other morning. I've been working with her for over a year, doing everything I can think of to get her out of her occasional bed of depression. I've sent newsletters, called her, taught her, and inspired her. She's had The Dream, but it's been fuzzy. Yesterday she said,

"Venus, I've been thinking about this for a week. Remember when I came to see you at 8:00 a.m. last Tuesday to get some product?" I nodded. "I can't forget it," she stated. "I was in a rush to get to work, I didn't want to go, and I was feeling frustrated and emotional. There you sat, tipped back in your recliner, wearing your red bathrobe, with your hair sprung out all over your head and no make-up at eight in the morning, drinking a cup of tea and chatting with me, just as relaxed and happy as you could be! I've thought about that all week! You've finally pushed me over the edge into really doing this business!"

"Well," I said, thinking of the sight I'd been, no lipstick and no charm to speak of, "If that's what it took to move you, thank God you saw me at my *best*."

"Yes," Sybyl agreed. "I want to be just like you: get up when I please, dress as I please, live my own life!"

I wish for all of you that your MLM business will bring you your freedom — that you'll have the time I've got to live your dreams, sit in the sun, eat crackers at midnight, and look like me in the morning....

"But how," you might say, "— the truth now Venus — do you get this freedom?"

How Do I *Really* Build This Business?

After reading my books, being trained by me, going to home meetings, company trainings, and reading various company and MLM materials, some people still say to me, "But, Venus, what do I do? How do I build this business?" Then they dance out a string of negatives about everything they've tried or thought about that hasn't worked. My answer is always the same:

"Stop thinking about it. Stop blaming yourself or outside forces. Stop complaining and crying and wondering. Just jump in and DO! DO! DO! DO! Even if you don't know what you're doing, do *something*. If it doesn't work, reevaluate, then jump in and do some more. Never give up. Keep persisting. Sometimes you'll feel like a rat on a roller, trotting along but never getting anywhere, but keep going."

An old couple called me the other night. I don't know them and they're in another MLM, but they had the same questions. They were discouraged. They'd been working their business for ten months and had two managers under them and only a few distributors. Nobody was doing anything. I could hear the old folks banging around their kitchen as they spoke with me over their speaker phone. "How can we motivate our people?" the wife begged as I heard a cupboard door slam.

"You can't," I said flatly. "If you've taught them everything you know and kept after them and they're not doing anything, it's not your fault. They don't have *inner* motivation. You do. Look for new people."

"But," they both wailed, "we should be doing better by now. So-and-so is making such-and-such a month and we're not. Lots of people in our company have big groups and big checks, and we feel like failures."

"Oh," I said, "how long have these people been in MLM? Ten years? Twenty?"

"Ah, well...yes," the old couple admitted, "most were in other companies before this one...."

"And you've only been working ten months," I ask, "at your first MLM?" There was a silent spell as light cleared the dark spaces in their collective heads. "Keep working," I advised. "Keep going to meetings, keep looking for the right kinds of people, and keep practicing this business. If you stick with it, you'll make it, and surely a lot sooner than ten or twenty years."

Be willing to start your business all over again if you have to. Sometimes, like bread dough that doesn't rise, you have to toss the batch and start again from scratch. Only this time, you know more. Revamp, revise, and get new people. You'll make fewer mistakes, and in the end, you'll be collecting blue ribbons, and big checks.

Will You Make It in MLM?

I'm thinking now of some top MLMers in our company: One man reeks of the farm. He's a "Hi-how-are-ya," good old boy; everyone feels comfortable with him. Another man is a powerhouse of purpose, but looks funny in his tight pants and dime-store shirt.

A homemaker who never worked at a "real job" is still sweet to everyone and bakes cookies every Tuesday. I work out of my kitchen. If you met me you'd say "She's a nice lady," and let it pass.

There are many more of us, unique in our own way, but not impressive unless you know who we are and what we accomplish. What do we, and all successful MLMers, have in common? We never let anything throw us out of the business. We never quit. We believe in what we're doing, and we keep doing it, no matter what or who is tossed in our way. Some of us feel that MLM is a form of life training and are glad for the teacher. Others of us don't consciously know it, but stay to learn, anyway.

Many people quit this game. They have all kinds of excuses. They lie to themselves. They pull out before the laps are run. If you're that kind of person, you'll pull out, too. If you're looking for" easy," either in life or in MLM, I can say good-bye to you right now.

I wish you well, but it's good-bye, because you won't find me, or any of the determined ones, dropping by the wayside to keep you company and chat. We're on a mission with many branches. We believe in what we're doing for ourselves and for others. We're aiming for the top, professionally and in our inner growth. We're resolute. Nothing will stop us. That's why we make it. You can, too. Will you?

Love,

Venus

To contact Venus, write:

c/o Ransom Hill Press
P.O. Box 325
Ramona, CA 92065-0325

Please enclose a self-addressed, stamped envelope
(SASE), and your phone number.

*For information on **motivational audio tapes** and other*
books by Venus, please write to the above address.

Venus counsels people for success in multilevel and is
*available for **motivational lectures**.*

———※◆※———

SAVE $$$
on
MLM MAGIC

You can save BIG when you order
multiple quantities of this book.
See Page 265.

———※◆※———

Information and order blanks for this book
and other Ransom Hill Press publications
are in the following pages. ☞

ORDER BLANK

Books & Tapes By Venus
Ransom Hill Press Books

_____MLM Magic..$16.95____ ____

_____MLM Magic (In Spanish) ....18.95_____

_____MLM Magic Workbook...................................18.95_____

_____Prospecting...12.95____ ____

_____Bad Blues...13.95_____

_____NetWorking Girls ....CALL FOR PRICE

_____Money Out of Control Audio.............................9.95_____

_____"Dear Venus" Letters   Vol I__Vol II__ .... 5.95_____

_____The Herb Lady's Notebook ....16.95_____

_____The Outrageous Herb Lady..............................12.95_____

Successful Women in Network Marketing Conference

_____Venus Andrecht - Audio Tape..⎫........................12.95 _____

_____Anne Boe - Audio Tape...........⎬ Buy 2 Get 3rd Free 12.95_____

_____Doris Wood - Audio Tape.........⎭........................12.95____ ____

Tax _____

Shipping _____

Make Checks Payable to: Total _____
Ransom Hill Press
P.O. Box 325 * Ramona, CA 92065-0352
CA Residents add Sales Tax

<u>SHIPPING</u> $3.00 for 1st Book, $.50 for each Additional Book
Priority Mail - $4.50 for 1st Book, $.50 2nd Book
Outside the USA, UPS & C.O.D - Please Call for Correct Amounts

_____Payment Enclosed

Credit Card #_____ Expiration Date _____

Name_____ Phone (   ) _____

Address _____

City_____ State_____ Zip_____ _____

1-800-423-0620
US & Canada
(619) 789-0620 Out of USA
FAX (619) 789-1582

All Prices Are Subject to
Change Without Notice

DISCOUNT SCHEDULE	
Mix & Match	
1 Item	0% off
2 - 3	15% off
4 - 5	20% off
6 - 10	25% off
11 - Up	30% off

Call for Larger
Discounts & Specials

VISA   Master Card   DISCOVER   AMERICAN EXPRESS

Glossary

800 Numbers: A service you can apply for from major telephone companies. You pay for long-distance calls from clients at a reduced rate.

Blind Ad: An ad in which the business of the advertiser is not revealed.

Bulk Mail Permit: A permit obtained from the post office which allows you to send mailing pieces at a reduced rate. The charges, at this writing, are: $75 initially, plus $60 per year.

Commitment: A promise to yourself and others that you will devote your time and energy to fulfilling a specified obligation.

Conference Call: A service provided by telephone companies which allows you to connect three or more parties in one telephone call. (You could hook yourself and your downline together on one call.)

Conventional Marketing: The usual method of selling goods through a retail outlet.

Direct Marketing: Selling products directly to the consumer through: door-to-door, telephone sales, parties, demonstrations, media, mail, etc.

Distributor: A person you have signed into the business under you.

Downline: All the people with whom you have shared the product and who have signed into the company (becoming a distributor, like you) and all the people that these people have shared the product with and signed into the company...and so on.

Dysfunctionals: People who do not function normally, for whatever reason. Dysfunctionals are sometimes children of alcoholics or from other abusive and odd families. Dysfunctionals are those of us who are driven, compulsive, obsessive, hysterical, recovering alcoholics, recovering drug addicts, recovering sex addicts, etc.

Entrepreneur: One who organizes, manages and takes the risk of a business.

Frontline: The distributors you have signed under you, or who have moved directly under you as others dropped away.

Hand-out: Any type of advertising handed out to individuals or left for them to find, such as: business cards, flyers stuck in car windshields, on walls, in phone booths, on public benches, etc.

Leg: One of your distributors and all of their downline.

Mail-order Marketing: Selling product by mail, mailing out promotional literature, such as catalogs, flyers, etc.

Manager: A person who has recruited downline to work under him/her. May also be called supervisor, or some other distinctive title.

Mentor: A trusted counselor, guide, tutor, coach.

MLM: Multilevel Marketing, or Network Marketing, consists of distributors several levels deep who distribute product for a specific comapny. Profits come from commissions on direct sales and money or royalties earned on sales made by the network of downline distributors. (Do not confuse with a pyramid scheme.)

Network: An interconnected or interrelated group of people who work together and help each other.

Newsletter: A letter or small newspaper directed to a special group.

Product: Something produced for sale.

Prospect List: A list of people who might potentially buy and/or sell your product.

Pyramid Scheme: A marketing scheme based on recruiting distributors, not to sell product, but to sell a place in the pyramid. Distributors are paid for the number of distributors recruited and not for product sold.

Retail Customers: Those who buy product from you on a regular basis, but do not wish to sell it.

Sales Reps: Salesmen/women who represent a company and go from store to store promoting and selling product to the merchants.

Sideline: People in other groups, unrelated to your group, but in the same company.

Speaker Phone: A telephone which has a device that allows telephone conversations to be amplified through a speaker (and not just the handset). (Any number of people within range can hear and speak to the party(ies) on the other end of the connection.)

Sponsor: A person who signs another person directly under him/her in a multilevel business.

Upline: All distributors above you, including the person who recruited you.

Voice Box: A telephone communication system which records messages.

Bibliography

Andrecht, Venus. *The Outrageous Herb Lady; How To Make A Mint In Multilevel Marketing.* Ramona, CA: Ransom Hill Press, 1990.

————. *The Herb Lady's Notebook, An Outrageous Herbal.* Ramona, CA: Ransom Hill Press, 1984, 1991.

Babener, Jeffrey A. *Tax Guide for MLM/Direct Selling Distributors.* Portland, OR: Legaline Publications, 1988.

————. *The Network Marketer's Guide to Success.* Portland, OR: Legaline Publications, 1990.

————. *The MLM Corporate Handbook.* Portland, OR: Legaline Publications, 1991.

Bly, Robert W., & Gary Blake. *How To Promote Your Own Business; Your Practical Primer To The Ins And Outs Of Advertising And Publicity.* New York, NY: A Plume Book, 1983.

Boe, Anne. *Is Your Net-working?* New York, NY: John Wiley & Sons, 1990.

Covey, Stephen R. *7 Habits of Highly Effective People.* New York, NY: Simon and Schuster, 1991.

Eisenberg, Ronni, & Kate Kelly. *Organize Yourself.* New York, NY: MacMillan Publishing Company, 1986.

Failla, Don. *MLM, EVERYTHING You Need To Know To Build A Large Successful Organization.* Edited by Joe Hardwick. Gig Harbor, WA: Joe Hardwick, 1986.

Givens, Charles. *Wealth Without Risk.* New York, NY: Simon & Schuster, 1988.

Gregory, Helen. *How To Make Newsletters, Brochures & Other Good Stuff, Without a Computer.* Sedro Wooley,

WA: Pinstripe Publishing, 1987.

Holtz, Herman. *Mail Order Magic.* New York, NY: McGraw-Hill, 1983.

Hutten, Shirley, with Constance deSwann. *Pay Yourself What You're Worth; How to Make Terrific Money in Direct Sales.* New York, NY: Bantam Books, 1988.

Kay, Mary. *Mary Kay, The Success Story Of America's Most Dynamic Business Woman.* New York, NY: Harper and Row, 1981.

Lowe, Janet. *The Super Saver; Fundamental Strategies For Building Wealth.* Whiteplains, NY: Longman Financial Services Publishing, 1990.

Phillips, Michael, & Salli Rasberry. *Marketing Without Advertising; Creative Strategies For Small Business Success.* Berkeley, CA: Nolo Press, 1988.

Robbins, Anthony. *Unlimited Power, The Way To Peak Personal Achievement.* New York, NY: Ballantine Books, 1986.

Schreiter, Tom. *Big Al's Turbo MLM.* Houston, TX: KAAS Publishing, 1988.

Snodgrass, Tod J., & Dr. Charles J. Jackson. *How To Save Up To 50% On: Office Supplies & Furniture • Business Forms & Printing • Office Machines & Equipment.* Torrance, CA: Lowen Publishing, 1985.

Winston, Sandra. *The Entrepreneurial Woman; How She Thinks & Copes; How She Succeeds In Her Own Business.* New York, NY: Newsweek Books, 1979.

Winston, Stephanie. *Getting Organized; The Easy Way To Put Your Life In Order.* New York, NY: W. W. Norton & Co., 1978.

————. *The Organized Executive; New Ways To Manage Time, Paper and People.* New York, NY: Warner Books, 1983.

Notes

Notes

Notes

Notes

"I found the book to be on the *'must read'* list for those interested in network marketing. If you're a beginner, you'll need this information. If you're an old pro, you'll enjoy the information, humor, and insight given by someone who has stepped into the arena and can be counted as one of us.

"*MLM Magic* is a fresh approach to the *'how to'* books on MLM. It gives you an idea of what it is like to start out in this business without 'heavy hitter' contacts, and it tells you what it takes to make your downline work. This is all presented by someone who has had her share of hard knocks in life, yet the humor in her life has never died. Anyone engaged in MLM knows the value of humor."

— *Robert W. Hahn*
President, Horizons Marketing Group, Inc.

"*MLM Magic* is a marvelous book that helps you deal with the *real* world of network marketing. Our people have had *great* success in building their businesses quickly and effectively. Quite simply the BEST book about network marketing!"

— *James and Karen Justice*
Double Diamond Distributors, Cell Tech

"*MLM Magic*—a **must** in preparing you for the rejections or discouragements that can happen early on in network marketing. I wish I'd had this book when I first started—I could have built this business bigger and faster."

— *Lydia Natividad*
Executive Director, Excel

MLM MAGIC

"*MLM Magic* should be part of any MLMers library. Whether you're just starting in network marketing or you're a seasoned pro, reading it is definitely the first step towards achieving success and financial independence."

— *Jeff & Tammy Carello*
National Training Directors, Excel

"Written by Venus Andrecht, an MLM pro who has done it herself, this book reads like you are talking to your best friend! If you're involved in MLM now or thinking about becoming involved, *MLM Magic* is the one book you should read right now."

— *Al Galasso*
North American Bookdealers Exchange

"When I read *MLM Magic* I realized immediately that Venus Andrecht knows what she is doing. She is obviously experienced and successful at network marketing. Her style is encouraging and fun as she *naturally* recruits and supports others on their way to success. Because of her natural and caring approach, I want every downline builder in my group to own and learn from her book."

— *Rich Hosking*
Double Diamond Distributor, Cell Tech
Relay Team 2000 Trainer